Marketing
Automation
Foundation

Eliminating Unproductive Marketing

By

Steve Thomas

&

Brian Thomas

Self-Published by

Steve Thomas

&

Brian Thomas

1795 Riverstone Drive
Delaware, Ohio 43015

Third-party trademarks and brands are the property
of their respective owners.

Book Edited by Beth Sharb

Book Cover Design by Brian Thomas

Illustrated by Danielle M. Dake

ISBN 9781521309247

Printed in the United States of America
May 2017

First Edition

Table of Contents

Who Should Read This Book

This book was written as an overview of digital marketing automation. It introduces software tools and concepts that will help those not familiar with marketing automation get started. If you are a small business owner or work at a medium sized company that isn't actively engaged in automation, this book will be a good starting point.

If you are a seasoned marketer who actively advertises online, this book will review familiar tools and concepts, as well as what the future of marketing automation holds. We hope you enjoy reading!

Preface

Brian and I wrote this book to introduce marketing automation to our friends, many of whom are also our customers. While working on various marketing projects, a recurring theme began to emerge. We found most people know about digital marketing and have a basic understanding of how it works. They understood how to write good blog posts, design beautiful graphics, shoot interesting videos, and create eye-catching ads. Most were very comfortable flying around the internet and social media as if they were playing a video game, particularly the millennials.

Yet, most had little knowledge about marketing automation and the effect it was having on marketing ROI. We found ourselves spending the first few sessions explaining the extent to which social media platforms were automated, under what circumstances they would use bots, and the role of artificial intelligence in marketing. As an example, we need to look no further than the U.S. Presidential election of 2016 to understand where marketing automation and technology is headed. The Russians, in an effort to sway the election, used an extensive network of Twitter bots, strategically timed posts, and social media knowledge to attempt to send their messages to the top of social media newsfeeds. Newsflash: it worked!

Virtually every marketing process is being automated, from advertising campaigns to lead generation and customer engagement. We track every click, page visit, comment, and social media platform people visit. Search engines and social media companies not only track everything we do online, but ultimately use that information – along with bots and artificial intelligence – to help companies actively seek and engage prospects.

It's no surprise that social media companies make the bulk of their money from advertising. It is a simple, yet brilliant, business model. The product they sell is access to you and me. When we sign up for Facebook, we create a profile describing ourselves. We give them our name, address, phone number, email address, where we live, our age, where we went to school, what we like to do for fun, the organizations we are members of, you get the idea. All for free! Then, each time we sign up for a newsletter or click on a free download while using our Facebook ID, we're leaving a copy of our profile behind.

Social media companies not only capture a staggering amount of personal data; they have developed their own libraries of marketing automation software. Have you ever noticed that most of the ads you now see are for products you're interested in? Advertisers are no longer wasting money promoting their products to people who have absolutely no interest in purchasing.

Marketing is more accurate and far less wasteful.

The days of *"spray and pray"* marketing are gone. The current suite of automation tools, such as Customer Relationship Management (CRM) systems, email service providers, and automated social media advertising tools, are just the beginning. Many businesses have already started experimenting with artificial intelligence, as well as bots that carry on Twitter conversations that can be indistinguishable from a real person. *Scraping* software, which searches websites and social media for specific words and phrases, is also starting to emerge as a lead generation tool.

Marketing automation has become so important to digital marketing that many companies have created a position known as the Chief Digital Officer (CDO). A CDO is a combination of both a Chief Marketing Officer and a Chief Technology Officer. Senior marketing executives need to be as familiar with technology as they are with marketing strategy.

If you are interested in digital marketing automation, this book is the first step in your marketing automation journey. You'll start by learning about the technology that makes marketing automation possible. Then, you'll discover some of the automation tools that prominent social media channels use and where the future of marketing automation is heading. Our goal is to give you an introduction to marketing automation by describing the new tools and tactics for your digital marketing practice. This book is the first step in eliminating your unproductive marketing.

Chapter: 1 Introduction

"Not implementing a marketing automation solution may be the ultimate career-limiting move for today's marketers."
– IDC Group

Welcome to the Party

I've always liked parties. Throwing them, hosting them, planning them; I make sure people have a good time. In college, I was the social chair of my engineering fraternity. After college, I ran the Columbus chapter of the alumni association for my alma mater, Virginia Tech. I've even held a few private events at my apartment overlooking the Arts District downtown. After dozens of events under my belt, I know how to throw a party.

Several years ago, I was in between jobs when an opportunity to throw a fundraising event presented itself. I jumped at the idea of throwing my first event as a "professional." It was the first time I'd turned a hobby into a job. With gusto, I set out to plan an event like I always had: find the venue, feature some guests, provide entertainment, set the scene, and personally invite everyone. It worked!

I thoroughly enjoyed it from beginning to end; the excitement, the people, the organizing, the stress. I found something I loved doing, and I knew I wanted to keep the momentum going. So, I threw a second event. It was even more successful than the first in attendance and execution. Boosted by lots of compliments and a few bucks in my pocket, I felt like I was a pro. But I was wrong.

At that point, it didn't matter. I was moving forward anyway. I formed an event planning and promotion company under the name Impact Social. With help from Steve, we created a business website, became active on social media, and started promoting events. For the first Impact Social event, we tried a new tactic: digital marketing. We mostly leveraged social media by creating posts about the upcoming event. However, it didn't take me long to realize that social media is not a field of dreams. "If you build it, they will come" is a fantasy many digital marketers believe when they start out. I was no exception. The only people who came to the third event were those personally invited. Exactly zero people showed up because of digital marketing. If you ever want to know embarrassment, make sure to throw a fundraiser for an in-need non-profit and then generate less than $50 for them. Not a good start.

If I was going to build a business that depended on getting paying customers through a door, I knew I couldn't just rely on my friends to fill the space. There were a few things that needed to be done. I needed to expand my network, motivate people to attend my events, and encourage guests to come back. I realized that there was a big difference between being an event planner and being in the event promotion business. I had to get creative.

Steve and I sat down and contemplated how to tackle this problem. One thing was obvious – we needed to figure out how to find people in Columbus who would be interested in attending our events. Buying a list wasn't an option. I'd tried this route before in business development roles and quickly realized it was a more harmful than helpful. It turns out people don't like to be nonconsensual solicited through email. We needed a way to not only reach an audience, but curate interest from an audience outside of my personal network.

I started promoting heavily on social media. Twitter, Instagram, and Facebook were my channels of choice. Tweeting and posting were helping keep the events in people's minds so they were more likely to sign up and attend. However, we still needed a way to find out who was attending these events so we could promote future events. We also needed to figure out what our best methods of promotion were, because they were starting to work.

Luckily, Steve has a master's degree in computer science, years of expertise in information technology, and a solid understanding of software programming. We created a database system that would capture names and emails of attendees whether they paid online or filled out our e-form at the door. It was the first version of our Customer Relation Management (CRM) system.

The Impact Social network started to grow when we became more aggressive with social media promotion and introduced the CRM system. I would throw fundraising events for nonprofits in various industries (specifically fashion, art, environmental, and young professional networking). Each of the organizations had a different network. We built web forms that captured the information of attendees, but just as importantly, it captured what types of events each guest was interested in. The information was captured by our CRM, which was now capable of separating attendees by interest, demographics, and industry for target marketing. Each industry was approached with different promotions for different events. Very rarely would I solicit the entire Impact Social network.

Soon, more organizations approached me for not only event planning, but marketing services as well. By this time, Steve and I had put together systems for email marketing, Facebook event syncing, cross-platform promotion, and e-commerce. Each of these digital marketing activities were necessary if I wanted to fill events.

I soon realized that event planning was a very small part of my new business. Yes, it was the face everyone saw, but the time it took to organize and create an event was nothing compared to the time, energy, and organization it took to promote the events. Impact Social was in the marketing business.

Automation Is Changing the Fundamentals of Marketing

It seems odd to make a statement about automation as if it's something new to marketing. After all, some of the most advanced software applications available are for marketing. Just look at Adobe's Photoshop–it seems like it's been around forever. Is there anyone under the age of 65 who doesn't know what Photoshop is, even if they have never used it? Very rarely do we run across someone who considers themselves in the marketing business who doesn't own or subscribe to Adobe Creative Suite. Their software is not cheap, but they have virtually everything you need to create graphics, design documents, create videos, and build websites. So, when it comes to creating great content, marketing software is no laggard.

Yet, when it comes to software that automates marketing processes not related to creating content, marketing is way behind. Banks, insurance companies, and even the Federal government started automating their basic operational tasks back in the 60s and 70s. Marketing has just recently gotten into the automation game.

This is probably no accident. Marketers strongly believe that the key to great marketing is great content. With all the marketing noise, your content had better stand out. It doesn't matter how many people you reach with your crappy content, because no one will care. For all the right reasons, creating great content has been the driver of marketing technology.

However, there are other technical aspects of marketing not related to creating content. It's about finding people who may be interested in buying your products. It's about understanding your customers, their behavior, their interests, and their likes and dislikes. It's about creating an environment where customers feel free to ask questions that will be responded to right away. It's about automating those activities that make marketing great content to the right people possible.

Automation Benefits

Our formal definition of marketing automation is "a category of software designed to automate marketing processes." This is absolutely true, but the definition doesn't provide any insight as to what marketing automation actually does. It can be as simple as installing a select button on a web page or a complex as a Twitter bot that includes artificial intelligence with natural language processing. It can mean installing a CRM or analytics systems. It also covers a wide range of software tools and marketing channels.

Software that includes elements of artificial intelligence is changing the fundamentals of marketing. While it's still the art of persuasion, the delivery and management of marketing is increasingly reliant on automation. We already have automation that makes highly precise target marketing possible, as well as software that includes predictive analytics, bots, and artificial intelligence. Virtually every marketing process is being automated, from advertising campaigns to lead generation and customer engagement. We're tracking every click, page visit, comment, and social media platform. Marketing automation is not only tracking everything we do online, but using intelligent bots to actively seek and engage prospects.

These are some of the benefits:

- **Tracking Advertising Campaigns** – Whether you use Google or social media, each platform has automated target marketing tools that make precision marketing possible. In addition, they track virtually every conceivable statistic about your campaign. A/B testing and agile marketing techniques are expected and built into the automation process.
- **Productivity** – Marketing automation is converting manual processes into automated processes, thus freeing the marketing staff to perform the more creative tasks of content creation and strategy.
- **Increase Revenue** – While creating software that automates revenue generation isn't cheap, it's generally well worth the investment. Consider this: B2B marketers see an average of 20 percent increase in sales from automation. Over 78 percent of high-performance marketers identify marketing automation as a key contributor to increasing revenue. By 2020, it is expected that 85 percent of customer relationships will be managed without human intervention.[i]
- **Targeting** – Whether it's social media or data from your CRM, there is a glut of tools that automate target marketing. Platforms like Facebook segment their users by groups, behavior, interest, demographics, and a variety of other categories. Target marketing on Facebook is simply a matter of checking off those you want to receive your content. Wasting time and money advertising to people who are probably not

interested in what you are selling is significantly reduced.[ii]

The benefits of automation are almost endless. Just automating email responses to customer inquiries is a big timesaver. As we move into the future, marketing departments will be dominated by programmers, mobile app developers, and social media experts. Successful marketing will depend on a company's technical agility as well as their ability to create great content.

The Evolution of Marketing Automation

Marketing automation has been around for as long as the internet, but in a much simpler form than we see today. It's common for people interested in what you sell to visit your website, view your Facebook business page, call you by phone, and read your Tweets. They may already be customers or even people who found their way to your website looking for something they want. Rest assured, your sales organization wants to know who these potential leads are. They want to know when and where they touch your business. They want to know what pages they visited and what social media platforms they use. They want to know as much as possible about those leads so they can turn them into customers.

Genesis

In the early days, marketing automation was synonymous with email marketing. This meant acquiring a list of email addresses, learning how to execute a mail merge, and continually scrubbing the mailing list for outdated addresses. As the market grew, several companies such as Constant Contact and MailChimp sprung up with fully automated email systems. They had a database for storing email address, names, and demographic information. Just as important, email service providers were good at keeping your business off the "*spammer*" blacklist. They were also good at capturing statistics on how well each of your email campaigns performed. Email service providers are still going strong, delivering an important marketing service.

In addition to email, web forms began to emerge as a marketing automation tool as well, capturing names and contact information from people visiting our website. Forms appeared on landing pages, "contact us" pages, and newsletter signups. The inclusion of web forms introduced one of the most valuable digital marketing assets ever created: the organic marketing list. People are willing to give their names and contact information because they have interest in what is being offered. Those receiving a marketing email from businesses they willingly gave their name to are 10 to 40 time more likely to open the email than emails they receive from being on a purchased list.

Evolution

As the internet grew, people became comfortable with using their credit cards, which grew online sales transactions. Sales departments became interested in the internet as a new distribution and prospecting channel. Companies wanted to know who was coming to their website and what they were interested in. Salespeople didn't have an interest in how many visitors came to their website; they wanted qualified leads. They needed names, contact information, and what pages those leads visited.

This is when Customer Relationship Management (CRM) systems started to move out of the sole domain of sales and became a marketing tool as well. They automatically captured demographic information, customer interests, carts filled, purchases made, and user profile information.

Prior to CRM systems becoming an internet marketing tool, entering names and other information was, for the most part, a manual process. By moving CRM systems online, marketing could automatically capture lead information. This meant sales could follow leads from the first visit to the final sale. CRMs began to do more than automatically capture information about leads; they introduced *customer segmentation* algorithms that separated people by interest and *scoring* technology that graded their likelihood to buy.

Ecosystem

The ability to automatically capture a prospect's online behavior started to blur the lines between sales, marketing, and technology. While the internet started out as the domain of marketing, product sales and lead generation made salespeople equally as interested. Websites became a major sales distribution channel and it was the automation created by marketing that made it happen. Yet, as we know, the internet didn't stop growing, nor did it stop spawning other marketing channels. Social media exploded onto the scene.

It's hard to believe, but it wasn't until 2007 that smartphones emerged. The first iPhone wasn't shipped until April of 2007. Social media was just starting to emerge as well. Facebook was around, but mostly on college campuses. Smartphones and social media were not part of our vocabulary. No Twitter, Instagram, Pinterest, Snapchat, or Vimeo (LinkedIn started in 2003). Each of these emerging social media platforms also capture everything their users do, whatever they click, and wherever they go. They track everything. Behavioral information is extremely valuable to a business trying to perfect its marketing. Social media companies target businesses as their main source of revenue and became very business-friendly, certainly in terms of their automated marketing tools. In fact, many have created libraries of code and APIs for accessing data. They offer videos and detailed instructions on how to build applications for their platforms, all in the name of attracting businesses as customers. For those of you who are not familiar with programming terminology, API stands for Application Program Interface. It provides the tools and instructions for communicating with software.

Today, a broad marketing automation solution includes:

- Email system
- Web CRM
- Analytics and Predictive Analytics
- Social Media Target Marketing Automation
- Remarketing Automation
- Bid Management Software

- Automated Prospect Segmentation and Scoring
- Cross-Platform Content Placement

The ecosystem of marketing automation is a network of connected marketing channels and software that track customers' online behavior. We can capture information about prospects at every touch point, whether it's on a website, from social media, or via a phone call to our business. It helps us become exponentially more knowledgeable about our customers and even more educated about likely buyers.

Botnets and Beyond

In the marketing automation ecosystem, we have seen the growth of an automation network where data is captured at multiple customer touch points on multiple channels. We are also starting to see the growth of even more sophisticated marketing automation in the form of bots, botnets, and artificial intelligence. While bots have been around for a while, their prominence came to light during the 2016 presidential election. Bots were deployed not as thousands of independent software programs, but as a coordinated network (botnet) of automation software for promoting articles and posts to the top of the social media Newsfeeds.

Many businesses have looked upon their success with great interest and are trying to adopt similar practices. It's hard to deny the potential for businesses.

So, get ready, because businesses are starting to turn their attention to creating very intelligent bots that automatically find prospects, engage those prospects, and turn them into sales. Expect business to employ the same practices the Russians used in the 2016 presidential campaign. Twitter already has over 40 million bots; expect this trend to grow and permeate other marketing channels. We no longer *spray* out emails and *pray* something will stick. The future of online marketing is automated, targeted, and personal.

Personalization

Two additional benefits of marketing automation include the ability to personalize marketing and accurately profile individuals interested in what you're selling. It's no longer acceptable to waste money on people who have shown no interested in your products. If a person is interested in fitness and visits a website that sells running shoes, you can capture that visit. Within a few minutes, that person will see advertisements about running shoes. All our internet clicks are recorded and available for marketing if you know where to look and know how to gain access.

Google and social media platforms track our buying habits, interest, and political views along with all of the personal information we provide in our profiles. The same goes of CRMs; they capture personal and behavioral data as well. It's what makes Facebook, LinkedIn, and other social media platforms so valuable. They track everything. Many of the marketing automation concepts we present in this book focus on personalization.

Important Concepts

Throughout this book, we use several concepts that may not be familiar to all readers. Even if you are familiar with these concepts, it's best to define them so we are all on the same page.

Marketing Channels

Digital marketing channels include websites, email, Facebook, Twitter, Instagram, and other social media platforms. We consider each of these platforms a distinct marketing channel. Facebook attracts people interested in connecting with friends; Twitter attracts people interested in keeping up with comments about real-time events like sports, politics, and news. Each platform differs from the others and requires different tactics. Throughout this book, we will refer to these platforms as marketing channels.

Setup

We use the term *setup* to reference the fundamental facilities and services provided by each marketing channel. For example, the setup of a website will consist of web pages, contact forms, call-to-action buttons, ecommerce, and a CRM. Many of the automation tools we describe are specific to each channel's setup.

There are other automation tools that are specific to marketing and analytics. For example, Facebook has marketing automation tools for boosting posts and direct advertising. They also have other tools that monitor advertising campaign statistics. We make a distinction between the tools that are used to analyze marketing campaigns and tools designed to automate the setup.

Reach

Reach is a metric used by most social media channels to indicate how many people were able to view a particular post. When you see the metric *"reach"* listed along with other analytics, it will typically have an organic and paid version that describe how many people (both in and out of your network) were shown the post, regardless of if they actually noticed it. Extending your reach is an important goal and a good indicator of how well your content is being received.

CPC

Cost Per Click (CPC) is one of the primary model's social media companies use to charge for advertising. If you're running an ad on Facebook or any other social media channel, tens of thousands of people may see your ad. However, you only pay when someone clicks on the ad. This is a good strategy when you are trying to drive sales. You're only paying for people interested in your product.

CPM

Cost Per 1,000 Impressions (CPM) is another advertising payment option. Instead of paying each time someone clicks on your ad, you're paying to have the ad presented to lots of people, whether they take action or not. This a good strategy when you are interested in building brand awareness.

#hashtags

#hashtags are metadata tags used on social media platforms that connects content to other content using the same identifier or "tags." In essence, it's a system used to categorize messages and connect them with other messages that employ the same hashtag.

Hashtags can be words or phrases, but have two requirements. First, the hashtag must have a pound (#) sign in front of the tag with no spaces between. Second, if the hashtag is more than one word, it must not have spaces between normally separate words. The first pervasive use of hashtags was adopted by Twitter in 2007. It allowed users to search for messages and updates that had been categorized by the hashtags.

For example, let's say on Monday you decide to post a motivational Tweet and at the end of the Tweet assign the hashtag #motivationalmonday. Then, anyone doing a search on Twitter for #motivationalmonday will have the opportunity to find your tweet. It's a way of grouping posts.

Since its adoption by Twitter, many other social media platforms have adapted to use hashtags. Facebook even asks what tags are relevant to your event when you create one. No matter your industry, it's important to stay up to date with relevant hashtags so you aren't left out of the loop.

Book Layout

We use a few conventions in this book we hope adds to its readability. For example, a person who visits your website can be a customer, lead, prospect, viewer, or member. We didn't want to list each one of these nouns every time we reference the individual taking-action. Therefore, we chose to use "prospect" to represent the entire category. There's nothing sacred about prospects; it's just the noun we chose.

While the book is not formally divided into sections, there is an informal arrangement. Chapter 2, Eliminating Unproductive Marketing, and Chapter 3, Marketing Profile, are there to provide a foundation for the rest of the book. Chapter 2 introduces the forces affecting marketing and why they demand automation. Chapter 3 shows you how to create a marketing profile of your business. This chapter may seem out of place for a book on marketing automation, but we've found many small businesses spend time marketing on social media channels because they are familiar with it, not because they are the right fit for that channel. We also find it hard to give advice about what channels businesses should be using and how unless we understand some of the basics about why they think marketing on a channel is a good idea. Completing the questions in Chapter 3 will help you better understand how your business should approach each channel.

Chapter 4, CRM, and Chapter 5, Email Marketing, are two of the most well-known marketing automation tools. Web CRMs are the repository for customer and prospect information. While they historically have been used by salespeople to track prospects as they move down the sales funnel, web CRMs have become the backbone of marketing automation. Chapter 5, Email Marketing, presents email as both an automation tool and a marketing channel. Email was the first widely used marketing automation tool and is still an important marketing weapon.

Chapters 6 through 11 present the marketing automation software available for the most dominate marketing channels, such as your website, Facebook, and Twitter. Even if one or more of the channels do not match your marketing profile, we recommend you review it anyway.

Chapter 12, The New Marketing Ecosystem, summarizes the book and makes predictions about the near-term and long-term future of marketing automation.

Our goal is to lay out the blueprint for the current digital marketing ecosystem. Once you have this foundation, you will be able to start building your unique approach to digital marketing by implementing the automation tools that make sense for your organization. The first step to eliminating unproductive marketing starts on the next page.

Chapter 2: Eliminating Unproductive Marketing

"I know half of my marketing works, I just don't know which half" – J.C. Penny

We technical types like to talk about disruption, so much so that it becomes a career goal to have our names associated with new technology that changes a market. But marketing automation is more than a minor disruption; it is a strategic inflection point, or what Malcolm Gladwell called a "tipping point," that fundamentally changes marketing. Automation is disrupting the marketing industry in the same way the automobile disrupted the horse-drawn carriage industry. All of us have watched as social media and smartphones grew from non-existence in 2007 to marketing dominance. Yet these are only two of the forces that are creating a marketing automation tipping point. Now, let's step back and look at what's causing this disruption.

The Five Forces Creating the Tipping Point

Most marketing analysts will tell you that after 25 years, the internet is no longer considered disruptive. Almost every business has a website, markets online, and buys digital services. But what happens when the way people use the internet changes? What happens when the way they access the internet changes? Looking through a traditional lens will be of little assistance when several of those changes result in a massive disruption. Marketing channels that barely existed in 2007 now generate over $40 billion in annual advertising revenue. When this happens, traditional marketing tactics become obsolete. We need to understand the forces causing change and adapt accordingly. Otherwise, we risk perishing.

It would be much easier to deal with if there was only one major disruption. However, we are at a confluence of five major disrupting forces. They are:

- **Social Media** – Over 72 percent of the United States population is on Facebook, and millennials spend approximately 2.5 hours a day on social media alone. Facebook generated almost $27 Billion in revenue in 2016, most of which was for advertising. For a group of channels that didn't even exist at the beginning of this century, social media would be the definition of a disruptive technology.

- **Smartphones** – Approximately 77 percent of Americans own smartphones, which is up from zero in 2006. No one needs to be convinced that smartphones have been a game changer.

- **Entertainment** – Prior to the internet and the proliferation of broadband, most of our daily entertainment came from watching TV. While TV is still one of the primary sources of entertainment, it is quickly being surpassed by social media, online videos, and video games. I have two boys, ages 10 and 12, who only recently learned how to operate the cable TV so they could watch Simpsons reruns, yet they fly around the internet the way their parents surf TV channels.

- **Automation** – The software that's helping us deal with these disruptions is also a major contributor to the disruption. Automating target marketing, capturing analytics, and engaging followers has become necessary to find new prospects. In addition, the use of bots has already seen exponential growth; Facebook already has over 80 million bots and Twitter has over 40 million. This is only the beginning. Bots will become more pervasive and intelligent as time goes on.

- **Content Creation** - Each year for the past several years, we have created more content than the rest of human history combined. We are inundated with banners, videos, blog post, ads, emails, news, newsletters, text messages, and countless promoters trying to grab our attention. There is so much content and advertising that consumers block it out almost like white noise.

It's hard to determine exactly when the tipping points occur. For marketing automation, we have arrived at the tipping point or are close to it. But we can't wait until we are absolutely sure. Timing is everything. Starting early gives us time to experiment and make changes. If we are in catchup mode, mistakes are amplified and work days become longer.

Fortunately, companies such as Facebook and Google who are at the forefront of this disruption have recognized the importance of automation. They make their money from advertising, which motivated them to create a variety of easy-to-use marketing tools. They also provide software development environments for third-parties and marketers to write custom software.

Marketing Profile

The first step in your marketing automation journey is to create a marketing profile of your business. The profile is not meant to be a comprehensive marketing plan, but rather a synopsis of your current marketing strategy. The profile is used as a guide for determining which channels are the most important to your business, which automation tools you're currently using, and which tools you should be using. Chapter 3, Marketing Profile, is devoted to creating a profile. Once you complete the Marketing Profile, you'll have a one-page overview that describes the purpose of your marketing, target market, objectives, and strategy.

Considering the next chapter is devoted to creating a marketing profile, we will not go into more detail here. However, we highly recommend you take the time to create the profile. It has been our experience that most small businesses don't have a written marketing plan and can't articulate their marketing strategy. The profile is meant to be short, but answers important questions about your strategy, purpose for marketing, and your target market. Then, as you review each marketing channel, you will be able to determine whether it makes sense for your business to market on that channel. It also provides insight as to which automation tools are right for your business and which ones are probably a waste of time.

Channel Ranking

The next step is to determine which digital channels are relevant for your marketing. It's easy to say all channels are important, but the time and energy required to build a digital marketing program is not worth the effort if the channel doesn't fit your strategy or target market. The odds of generating a positive ROI through these channels becomes increasingly remote. For example, a software services firm may find prospects on Pinterest, but they are better off spending energy on their website, working on SEO, and advertising on LinkedIn. Pinterest is not a site where you are likely to find viewers interested in software services.

In Chapters 5-11, we review prominent marketing channels such as Facebook, Twitter, and your website. At the front of each chapter is a description of the channel, its demographics, and the audience it attracts. Use your marketing profile to compare and analyze the channel's fit for your business. When you finish reviewing all the channels, rank them and eliminate those that are not worth the effort. A sample LinkedIn Channel Description is provided below. You will find similar profiles in each chapter.

LinkedIn Channel Description

LinkedIn is a social media platform focused on business, employment, and professional networking. The company was launched in the spring of 2003 as a place for job seekers to post their resumes. Since then, it has grown into the world's largest professional networking site.

LinkedIn differs from other marketing channels because of its focus on employee recruiting. By encouraging users to create profiles that look like resumes, the channel provides marketers with one of the best company directories in the market. Profiles are set up to include positon titles, skills, current company affiliation, and education. LinkedIn is one of the few social media platforms that attracts many users over the age of 35. For B2B marketers, LinkedIn will be a top social media marketing channels.

On June 13, 2016, Microsoft announced plans to acquire LinkedIn for $26.2 billion. The acquisition was completed on December 8, 2016. The transaction resulted in the payment of approximately $26.4 billion in cash merger consideration.[iii]

Description	Results
Total LinkedIn Users	467 million
Active Users	109 million
Outside United States Users	70%
% of People by Age Group with Profile	
18-29	23%
30-49	31%
50-64	30%
65+	21%
Gender (as a % of the online population)	
Men	28%
Women	27%
% of People by Income Bracket with a Profile	
$75,000+	44%
$50,000-$74,999	31%

$30,000-$49,999	21%
<$30,000	15%
Education (Among Internet Users)	
College Graduate	50%
Some College	22%
High School or Less	12%
Revenue	$3.2 Billion in 2016

Table 2.1 Sample LinkedIn Channel Description

Emerging Automation Concepts

As we stated earlier, marketing automation is not confined to CRMs and email applications. It's emerging as an ecosystem of intelligent software for highly targeted marketing, capturing analytics, and software that automates many of the interactions between businesses and their customers. The marketing ecosystem is also an interconnected web of marketing channels, such as Facebook, websites, and YouTube. Each channel has its unique purpose and users. They also share information to create a comprehensive picture about customers and their impression of your products.

Emerging alongside the marketing ecosystem is a set of automation categories that are unique to marketing. Most of the automation tools we review fall into distinct categories such as target marketing, remarketing, and analytics (remarketing is described later on in this chapter). For example, Facebook has a variety of automation tools that are classified as target marketing automation tools, as well as other tools for remarketing, analytics, and bots.

Below we introduce these automation categories and describe the type automation tools that fit those groups.

Channel Setup

Each marketing platform has its own unique setup or infrastructure. As we review each channel, we describe what it takes to start using the channel and what is unique about its setup. For some channels, such as Twitter, setup is very simple and takes very little time. For others, such as a website, setup can be quite complex, time consuming, and offer a plethora of automation options.

The channel setup refers to those tools used to create, manage, and support your presence on the platform. For example, your website may have ecommerce for product sales, a Customer Relationship Management (CRM) system for capturing prospect contact information, and a plugin that syncs your site with Facebook events.

In addition, a platform such as Twitter is simple to set up, but also has a variety of automation software that can be added to your setup. They have a developer's environment for creating bots, as well as an abundance of automation software you can purchase from third parties.

Target Marketing

Target marketing is not a concept that needs to be introduced. However, you should be aware that for many social media platforms, their most advanced automation tools are geared towards target marketing. While they don't give you the names and profile information of individuals that you want to target, they will provide you the marketing tools to refine your selection criteria. Then, they will advertise to those who fit the criteria on your behalf.

Let's use Facebook as an example. Under their paid advertising tools, you can select your target audience by age, gender, location, and language. In addition, you can include people by demographics, interest, behavior, and Facebook categories. Still, it goes even deeper; you can drill down into demographics and select by education, financial bracket, life events, politics, and more. The same is true for interest and user behavior. The combinations aimed at selecting a target market for advertising or boosting a post are almost limitless.

Social media marketing tools are most certainly marketing automation tools. Consequently, as we review each social media channel, we spend more time on the automated tools for target marketing than anywhere else.

Analytics

To go along with targeted marketing tools, each channel provides numerous statistics about marketing campaigns, page visits, and followers. Social media channels are great at capturing marketing related statistics such as page visits, likes, shares, Tweets, retweets, and the number of comments made by visitors. They track everything. Facebook tracks over 250 individual statistics and makes them available for marketing analytics.

In this book, we present stories about how people used analytics that help improve their marketing to produce better outcomes. One of the most important features of automated marketing is the ability to capture and report analytics. Measuring the success of each campaign is the key to eliminating unproductive marketing.

Though the analytics differ from one channel to the next, there are several base statistics that are similar between channels. For example, if you are reviewing your business page's Facebook Insights (Facebook calls analytics "Insights"), you will see:

- Page Views
- Page Likes
- Reach
- Engagements

These four statistics are good indicators about how well your business page is performing on Facebook. They have similar statistics for page boosts and ads, such as:

- Reactions (Like, Love, HaHa, Wow, Sad, Angry)
- Post Clicks
- Link Clicks
- Comments
- Reach
- Shares

These are the base statistics that indicate how well your posts and paid ads are performing. However, if you have a programmer on your staff, more statistics can be captured for your CRM system.

You'll have access to information like the list of users who liked a particular post or a user's friends list. This is important if you need to capture campaign statistics, as well as names and contact information for your CRM.

Remarketing

Remarketing is a concept you are familiar with, even if you are not familiar with the name. Have you ever noticed after visiting a website that sells a product, you immediately start receiving ads about that or similar products? This is a rhetorical question because everyone has had this experience. The business selling the product, as well as the search engine that helped you navigate to that page, know what you viewed. They immediately start placing advertisements in front of you about that product or similar products. This is remarketing.

The most important notion about remarketing is that with automation, you can advertise to those who have shown recent interest or have interest right now. Automating the remarketing process could be one of the best revenue-driving strategies you can implement. You could also be identifying your best prospects.

Localization

There are two forms of localization. The first is localization associated with a city, region, or state. You can specify your advertising to be confined to your chosen location. If we choose Columbus for our Facebook advertising, then only people from Columbus will receive that advertising. This is particularly important to local businesses that depend on local traffic.

A second localization technology that's just starting to emerge is known as iBeacon technology. Generally, iBeacon technology is set up in a store, such as a grocery store. When you enter the store, you connect your phone to the iBeacon system. Then, as you traverse the aisles, your phone will receive advertisements, coupons, and information about products. While we don't review the iBeacon marketing technology is this book, we consider it an important emerging technology. We also expect it to become pervasive within the next couple of years.

Social Listening

There are a variety of software tools available for social media monitoring or social listening. These tools are designed to actively listen for mentions of URLs, hashtags, keywords, phrases, and ongoing conversations. The intent is to understand what is currently being said about your business, products, or topics of interest.

There are a variety of social listening software applications already on the market such *Keyhole,* which is used to track URLs, hashtags, keywords and usernames on Twitter and Instagram. *Bandwidth* is another that monitors over 80 million blogs, news sites, forums, and social media sites. *Google Alerts* is a simple tool for monitoring publications, keywords, news sites, and forums.

There are many social listening tools to choose from depending on your needs. The advantage of these tools lies in the fact that you can listen to what people are saying right now. It's great for monitoring trends as they happen or know what people are saying about your products.

User Generated Content

User Generated Content (UGC) is any content such as text, video, or audio that is created by a user. Think of it as content created by an amateur not a professional. As you create your digital marketing strategy, be aware that a recent study found that 85 percent of internet viewers would rather see UCG over brand photos or videos. Even more noteworthy is that shoppers were 97 percent more likely to purchase if they saw UGC than not.[iv] Marketers are taking note of this trend, so you should expect to see a significant jump in UGC in the immediate future. While UGC is not automation, the ability of a platform to easily manage and present UGC is. So, as we review various marketing channels, we will note the channel's ability to work with UGC.

Bots

A bot is computer software that is designed to perform repetitive tasks. For example, Twitter estimates that their users have created over 40 million bots to perform tasks such as carrying on conversations, acquiring followers, and automatically "liking" Tweets from their followers. Almost all social media platforms allow for bots and have development environments for creating bots. While bots have been around for a while, the 2016 Presidential election brought bots to the forefront.

If it's still a little confusing as to what a bot is, think of it this way. Your smartphone has apps that you download from either the iPhone or Android app store. Those apps can range from kid's games, sports channels, fitness monitoring, and rotating pictures of cats. The variety of apps are almost endless. Now, think of a bot as an app. Only you don't download the bot to your smartphone–you download it to your website, Facebook, Twitter, or Instagram. Instead of being a kid's game, they're performing business and marketing functions. The analogy is not exact, but it's close.

Bot software is not confined to any special kind of software or task. They can be built to do anything from the simplest to the most complex task. However, when it comes to collecting data from social media platforms, tracking trends, or searching blogs and websites for phrases, bots are very powerful. We expect the use of bots to continue to grow both for legitimate business as well as for nefarious purposes. We will point out channels where the use of bots makes sense and describe how they are used.

Artificial Intelligence

Artificial intelligence (AI) for marketing is an emerging marketing science that uses algorithms and database marketing techniques to engage prospects. What makes the software or bots intelligent is its ability to mimic human logic. For example, there are many bots on social media sites such as Twitter that can carry on conversations with live users, called *chatbots*. Embedded in the bots are algorithms that calculate what the user is saying and respond intelligently. Simple AI algorithms will have simple responses while more complex algorithms will have better responses (or so the theory goes).

There are a variety of uses for AI in marketing, such as sentiment analysis, voice recognition, and product recommendations. Ad targeting is another emerging AI area. Some companies have built AI software that optimizes the ad bidding process to find the best pricing (a form of programmatic marketing). In the future, chatbots are expected to replace some mobile apps for taking orders by phone. They will accept both voice and text to analyze orders using Natural Language Processing (NLP).

Most of us have already experienced marketing AI. If you're an avid reader and use an Amazon Kindle, you'll notice that every time you open your device there are new reading recommendations based on your reading habits. Audible does the same with audiobooks. Spotify, Pandora, Google, and iTunes do the same with music. The commonality of all these recommendations is that they are driven by AI. There is no proof that you will enjoy these recommendations. However, using predictive analytics and data gathered from others who have similar preferences, artificial intelligence is driving us to the products we want before we know they exist.

Predictive Analytics

A subset of AI is Predictive Analytics. This is the

science of using data to detect patterns and predict future behavior. For social media, predictive analytics is used to locate prospects with the intent to buy and predict what content they want to see. It can be used to predict almost any marketing activity in which data can be collected such as targeted advertising campaigns, personalization, and polling. However, the chief use is for sales and sales forecasting. Predictive analytics has also been used to forecast how well a post will perform on various social media platforms as well as make recommendations on which posts to boost.

We introduce predictive analytics because of its ability to analyze marketing data and determine the most likely behavior patterns of potential buyers. The way most businesses currently make decisions about who, where, and how they target, is done manually. They review the analytics produced from recent marketing campaigns and adjust accordingly. Adding predictive AI algorithms can uncover patterns that otherwise would go undetected. It's another automation tool that takes the guess work out of marketing.

Third-Party Cross Platform Automation Tools

Third party automation tools are popular among

marketers because they make it easy to create content in one location, before uploading it to multiple social media platforms. Most are offered as monthly paid or free services and provide a wide range of management and analytics tools. The tools we list below work across most major social media platforms. We decided to list them here rather than repeating them in each chapter.

- **Agora Pulse** – is for managing all your social media messaging in one place. It also includes statistics, reports, and how you stack up against your competition.
  (https://www.agorapulse.com/)

- **Hootsuite** – is a cross-platform tool for managing content, scheduling post, analytics, reports, and advertising across just about every platform. It's also good for finding and managing content. (https://hootsuite.com/)

- **Buffer** – focuses on scheduling and distributing posts across multiple social media platforms. (https://buffer.com/)

- **Oktopost** – is a cross platform tool for B2B social media marketing. It supports social media marketing strategy, publishing, extensive analytics, campaign management, and more. It's an expensive service, costing $400 per month. However, if you want to scale up your B2B social media marketing, it may well be worth the price. (https://www.oktopost.com/)

- **SocialBakers** – is a cross-platform analytics tool, providing comprehensive social media analytics along with reporting and a customizable dashboard. While it's not as expensive as Oktopost at $75 a month, they do offer a variety of analytics service that are worth a look. (https://www.socialbakers.com/)
- **DrumUp** – is a multipurpose social media tool, providing content location services, hashtag recommendations, and scheduling services. Its main focus is on content strategy and marketing execution. (https://drumup.io/)
- **Klout** – is a cross-platform tool for creating and sharing social media content. Similar to other cross platform tools, they provide content management, marketing services, and analytics. (https://klout.com/home)
- **Social Mentions** – is a keyword search tool. The service is quite simple–go to the social mentions website and enter your keyword or phrase. (http://www.socialmention.com/)
- **AdRoll** – is a tool focused on collecting and analyzing customer data. They consider

themselves the world's premier remarketing service. (https://www.adroll.com/)

- **HowSocialable** – is a service that measures the effectiveness of a brand or product across most major social media platforms. (http://howsociable.com/)

This list is by no means comprehensive—in fact, it is only the tip of the iceberg. In each of the social media chapters, we also list a variety of tools that are specific to that platform. The next chapter, Marketing Profile, is the most important in this foundation. It will help create a guide that will let you focus on the appropriate channels and tools you need to improve your marketing practice. Let's start building.

Chapter 3: The Marketing Profile

"Marketing is no longer about the stuff you make, but about the stories you tell."
– Seth Godin, Author

The first time we went through the process of creating a marketing profile was with James Gilmore, owner of The November Company, a film and video production firm. As is usually the case for small business owners, he was creating most of his own marketing with the assistance of one other part-time helper and an email marketing company. We thought this was going to be a simple and quick process. All we needed was straightforward answers about his marketing, such as: Who is your target market? What is your business identity? What marketing tools and channels do you use?

Right from the start, James became frustrated. He struggled to articulate most of his answers. Almost every question become a mildly stressful discussion. The session we thought would take an hour ended up taking almost three, and we still did not get through all the questions, even though there were only six. All we were trying to do was create a marketing profile. It was no more than a synopsis of The November Company's more detailed marketing plan. As it turned out, we were the problem.

After the meeting, our team went to a close-by watering hole to debrief and discuss plans for our next steps. When we brought up the observation that James seemed frustrated with the process, one of our team members provided some great insight. He said he had been in a similar situation once where someone was asking him similar questions – basic questions about his business that everyone should know. Yet, he said he struggled with the answers the same way James struggled. He knew he should know the answers and had a sense of what he should be doing, but could not clearly articulate the answers. There is a big difference between knowing your business and having the ability to communicate its intricacies.

The last thing we wanted to do was frustrate our client on the first real day of our engagement. Not a good way to start. In the case of James, everyone was fine and we continue to have a great relationship. When it came to small businesses, we found that James was not the exception, but rather the norm. As it turns out, it's rare for small businesses to go through an organized marketing planning process. They generally don't create a marketing plan, follow that plan, and track statistics. If they did, they probably wouldn't be talking to us. Small businesses generally don't have the time or resources to design, execute, and measure a serious marketing campaign. It is generally the last thing they consider as they work to get their businesses going.

The lesson we learned for our first few encounters was "don't surprise your customer." Provide them the agenda, questions, and the kinds of responses expected for each question in advance. Give them a chance to prepare. The result? Our clients were more engaged and less stressed. As you read our six marketing profile questions and find yourself struggling with some of the answers, remember – you are far from alone.

The Purpose of a Marketing Profile

We can take a lesson from social media when it comes to marketing. The first requirement upon signing up is to create a profile. They provide social media companies with details about you, your business, and your interests. With this information, they know what content you may be interested in and what advertising you may respond to. In the same spirit, the marketing profile is used as a guide to help you evaluate each marketing channel.

Profile Questions

The goal of a marketing profile is not to create a detailed marketing plan, but a synopsis that clearly defines a set of objectives for measuring progress. In most cases, one sentence should be enough of an answer for most questions. For example, the question "Who is your target market?" should have a response such as, "Our target market is females between the ages of 14 and 20 who are active and participate in sports." With this one sentence, you instantly have a reasonable idea about what marketing channels will be effective and which ones will not. Without any other knowledge, we know you are more likely to find more prospects on Facebook or Instagram and less likely on LinkedIn.

To create a one page marketing profile, we start with the following six questions:

1. Why do you market?

2. What marketing channels do you currently use?

3. Who is your target market?

4. What marketing tools & tactics are in use?

5. What is your business identity?

6. How do you measure success and allocate time and budget?

Each question is explained below.

Why Market?

"What is the purpose of your marketing?" In other words, "Why do you spend time and money on marketing in the first place?" Surprisingly, this question stumps most people. Why market your business? If you sell smartphones to the general public, then driving sales and creating awareness of your phones is the purpose of your marketing. If you are Boeing and sell commercial airplanes, the target buyer for your airplanes is very limited, consisting mostly of airlines and governments. Considering that their target market is so small and that their buyers are aware of Boeing, the reason for their marketing is not quite as obvious.

We are looking for a specific answer. To help, we have categorized the reasons for marketing. In most cases, you have more than one reason. Ultimately, businesses market to generate sales, but that's not good enough. The following is a list of marketing objects that will help you categorize why you market:

Build Awareness

- Generate excitement around a new product or service

- Establish an individual or business as an expert in their field

- Create interest around a specific topic
- Create media interest and coverage

Extend Reach

- Reach more prospects
- Generate leads
- Capture emails and build marketing lists
- Build a following of supporters, members, volunteers, or customers

Take-Action

- Buy a product, download a white paper, sign up for newsletter
- Volunteer or donate
- Attend a meeting, participate in a march
- Join a cause

Customer Retention

- Keep current customers happy
- Engage current followers with interesting content
- Generate feedback from followers

Generate Referral

- Get followers to share with their friends
- Start conversation and generate interest

Sales

- Drive revenue
- Drive prospects into your store

Build a Community

- Connect with people that have the same interest
- Create a community around a topic
- Build a following

The answer to the question "Why do you market?" may look like the following.

- The purpose of our marketing is to create awareness and drive sales for marketing services to local businesses.

- The purpose of our marketing is to drive donations and motivate people to act by volunteering.

In most cases, you should be able to define why you market in one sentence.

What Marketing Channels Do You Use?

Earlier we defined marketing channels as platforms that are used to promote and advertise businesses, products, and services. Once you define the purpose of your marketing, simply list the channels you are currently using. Only list those you use.

The following is a list of well-known marketing channels. This list is by no means complete. Given the proliferation of Internet platforms, digital marketing channels are constantly in a state of flux.

Well-Known Digital Marketing Channels

Website	Facebook	Twitter
Instagram	YouTube	Vimeo
Snapchat	Pinterest	Email
Google (AdWords)	LinkedIn	Periscope
Reddit	Flickr	Digg
Google+	Tumblr	Dribble

Table 3.1 Sample list of marketing channels

Target Market

From our experience, we find that answering the question "who is your target market?" is either the easiest or most difficult for people. Let's say you sell running shoes for long-distance runners. Clearly, your target market is runners. They may be range from world-class runners to weekend warriors. Figuring out what marketing channels to use and how to find where runners tend to congregate online is straightforward. Creating a marketing campaign that cracks the running shoe market is another matter altogether, but your target market is easily definable.

We also find businesses that sell services that could be used by everyone. Let's take The November Company as an example with video production. While James focuses on TV series and documentaries, he could also generate income from weddings, bar mitzvahs, and commercials. Any of these markets can use The November Company's services. However, the marketing programs they would use to target channels interested in a TV series is very different than the way they would market weddings. So, as a video production company, The November Company needed to decide. They can't be all things video to all people. Fortunately, James had a very clear idea about his target market. More often than not, people don't.

Your answer to the question of "who is your target market?" should have a clearly identifiable category of people. If you sell software to data centers, then your answer should read something like "Our target market is data center managers." Knowing specifically who to target in terms of job titles or interest, such as runners, becomes important when you use social media automated marketing tools.

The more specific you can be about your target audience, the better your marketing will be received.

Tools and Tactics

When we talk about tools, we are generally referring to the software applications you use for marketing. For example, to automate the email process, you may use MailChimp. Therefore, email is the channel and MailChimp is the tool. Here are some examples of other tool categories:

CRM System	Analytics Software	eCommerce
Event Marketing	Survey Management	Sales Insight Software
Lead Scoring Software	SEO	Web Forms
Bots	Marketing Campaign Software	Email Service Provider

Table 3.2 Automation Tool Categories

This is not a comprehensive list, but you get the idea. If you do an internet search on marketing automation tools, you will find that most sites focus on one of two key tools – a CRM system and email marketing. The reason these two categories of automation tools generate the most attention is that both focus on sales and generating sales leads. In addition, they have been around a lot longer than automation tools available on social media sites.

A tactic is different than a tool. For example, if one of your marketing purposes is to create awareness, then you may use the tactic of creating content to post on your website, blog, and Facebook. Creating interesting content is the tactic. Another tactic would be hosting events or seminars. Blogging is a tactic. Newsletters are a tactic. Creating controversial tweets on Twitter is a tactic. Podcasting is a tactic. They are not the tools, but rather what you do to market.

For this exercise, keep your answer at a higher level, such as "we have an aggressive social media content development strategy." The tactics you use will be addressed when you audit the individual channel.

What is Your Business Identity?

Your business identity is your brand. What do people think of when your company's name is mentioned?

- Cartier – High-quality jewelry.
- Microsoft – Affordable software.

- PWC – Professional consulting.

- Mercedes-Benz – High-end automobiles.

- Honda – Low-cost, high-quality cars.

- Spotify – Music streaming service

What position have you staked out in your market? You certainly have an idea about how you want to be perceived. However, ask your customers and friends about their perception. You may find that what you think is vastly different than what your customers think. Take their perception as a starting point because yours is where you want to be, but theirs is the reality.

Measuring Success

By measuring success, we mean setting goals. Have you set any marketing goals, such as the number of monthly qualified prospects? Have you set goals for each of the marketing channels you currently use, such as the number of visitors, membership sign-ups, followers, or conversions? We are not suggesting you set goals for every statistic, but if you have, what are they?

If you have already set goals, great! If you haven't, don't make up goals at this point. Wait until you finish your review of each channel. By then, you'll have a better understanding of what sort of marketing production you can expect. Eventually, you will set measurable goals for each channel.

We also ask that you specify how much time and money you spend on digital marketing. While it's not necessary to detail every expenditure, it will be valuable to have a good idea. For example, you may spend $30,000 and 60 hours a month advertising on Facebook. If you know it, include it. If not, find the person who does. Eventually, your success will be judged by the ROI. Getting a handle on expenditures and measuring success is important for determining progress.

Sample Marketing Profile

Sample is a software development company that builds Internet of Things (IoT) applications for large manufacturers. The software applications are designed to gather hard-to-get sensor data, track analytics, and deliver real-time information to operational managers to assist in making decisions that save time and energy.

Sample's services include consulting, software development, SAAS, and SCADA integration. The marketing IoT focus is on large manufacturing companies. However, Sample wishes to expand their technology development business to the healthcare industry and needs additional marketing efforts to penetrate the market.

- ## Why Does Sample Market?

    - o Sample's goal is to acquire a new audience, generate leads, and build an email list to drive sales.

- ## What Marketing Channels are Being Used?

    - o Website, LinkedIn, Facebook, Twitter, and YouTube.

- ## Who is Sample's Target Market?

    - o Sample's new target market is medium to large health organizations & hospitals. Within hospitals, they target CIOs, CTOs, and IT directors.

- ## What Automation Tools Does Sample Use?

    - o Sample uses Custom 7 Forms, website analytics plugin, woocommerce, Impact Social Media Stats, and MailChimp.

- ## What is Sample's Brand Identity?

    - o Sample's identity is a web software

development company, specializing in wireless products.

- **How Does Sample Measure Success, Time, Resources?**

  o Sample has analytics tracking on the website, each social media platform, and email marketing. One business development employee & 20k year marketing budget.

Brand Identity

Sample is perceived as a wireless company that sells wireless sensor devices. Some even confuse the company with wireless cell phone providers rather than a software services company focused on IoT systems. Others see the company as a high-tech company but are confused about details.

Conclusion

With your marketing profile ready, we will start looking at some of the commonly used tools and channels in the digital marketing ecosystem. We start with the CRM, which is the glue that holds all of the pieces together. From capturing social media data to automating email tasks, CRMs hold all of the information you will need to market once your foundation is built.

Chapter 4: Customer Relationship Management

"The purpose of a business is to create a customer."
–Peter Drucker, business management author

One evening, Impact Social was hosting an event for the non-profit organization Fashion Week Columbus. Fashion Week is an organization that serves as a platform to showcase local and emerging fashion designers, while also providing scholarships to fashion design students. People attending the event were fashion designers, manufacturers, models, and corporate apparel employees.

This was one of the first events thrown by Impact Social. In terms of greeting people and collecting donations, we were doing great. However, there were no systems in place to capture contact information from attendees. Impact Social had been contracted to hold a series of Impact Fashion events that stretched out over the next six months. We figured if the event was good, many of the attendees would probably want to know about other events, who was speaking, and where it was. While some people are reluctant about giving out their email address, most were willing.

For the next event, we wrote a simple software program that consisted of a web form. It only asked for a name and email address, then stored it in a database. When attendees entered the event, we told them why we wanted their email address. We asked if they would willingly provide this, and most did (it helped that anyone who gave their email was entered to win a bottle of liquor). This was the start of the Impact Social CRM.

The goal at that point was very simple: build an email marketing list. The bigger the list, the more direct marketing Impact Social could do to promote future events.

From there, we added more capabilities. We tracked what events people came to; we tracked what type of events interested them; we tracked how much they donated; if they paid with a credit card, we tracked that too.

The CRM gave us the ability to gather data and get smart about our customers. For example, Impact Social's analytics showed that 83 percent of those attending Impact Fashion events found out about the events from Facebook. 73 percent found our website through the mobile Facebook app and paid for the events online. The demographic also showed that over 50 percent of the Fashion event attendees were between the ages of 25-34. This information was invaluable in making Impact Social's marketing more effective.

The Backbone of Marketing Automation

If you're interested in marketing, you're probably not reading this book because of the obligation that comes with being a friend or family member. It's also highly likely that you have a decent idea of what a CRM system is. Historically, CRMs have been used by sales to manage their customers, prospects, and sales cycles. Over the years, CRMs began to add a sundry of modules for marketing, finance, and product support. Then, CRMs designed for the web started to track when, where, and how a customer interacted with a business's website.

Consider a web CRM to be the backbone of marketing automations. In this chapter, we explore CRM capabilities by asking a series of questions. Those questions go to the heart of a web CRM's abilities. We ask questions such as: Do you segment customers into categories? Do you score them on their likelihood to buy? Do you allow customers to build their own profiles on your website? These are some of the functions we find in a good web CRM. We also find that many organizations perform the same or similar activities manually or semi-manually using spreadsheets and custom databases. You need to identify these activities and replicate them in a web CRM system.

Make no mistake, CRMs are not an option. If you plan to automate marketing, a CRM is a requirement. CRMs perform many of the same automation functions you find on social media sites. They have the capacity to create profiles for their customers (and prospects) in the same way a social media channel does. They're capable of tracking clicks, page visits, and purchase made on your website in the same way Facebook tracks what you do on their site. With a CRM, you can replicate the same automation activities found on social media site.

Let's put things into prospective. On Facebook, you fill out a profile and they track your activity. On LinkedIn, Twitter, and Instagram you do the same. However, individual social media channels don't share profiles and activity information with each other.

Now imagine your CRM with the same capabilities, plus the ability to link profiles created on other social media channels. CRM profiles end up becoming the Master Profile because of their ability to track prospects across multiple channels. Once we sync profile information between channels, we can then track clicks, page visits, tweets, and other behavioral information as prospects move between channels. This is not future technology; it's already available but not widely implemented. It's marketing's version of big brother. CRMs will also serve as the foundation for future artificial intelligence base marketing and continue to be the backbone of the marketing automation ecosystem.

CRM Questions

Many small and medium-size business don't have a formal web CRM system. Yet most do, by one means or another, capture information about customers. If you are using a web CRM software package, you want to identify which functions you use and to what extent. If you don't have a web CRM, do you use website landing pages to capture prospect data? Are you including Facebook and other social media data to build your customer list? Do you segment customers for marketing purposes into groups? Do you use a scoring system to rate customers and prospects? None of these activities require a CRM software package, but it's certainly a lot easier if you have one.

We provide questions listed in *Appendix A, CRM* that are specific to a web or marketing CRM. Use these questions to identify the extent to which digital customer relationship management is being used. The intent is not to delve deeply into each function or CRM marketing practices. That would require a more in-depth CRM audit and is beyond the scope of this book. The sections below cover the most important questions and describes why they're important.

Do You Use a CRM?

The first five questions in the list are fairly straightforward and need little explanation. For example, in question 2, "Which modules or functionality are you using?" applies to those who have a web CRM. If you use a web CRM, the head of marketing should know which web CRM functions your business purchased. If you use a database, are you using SQL Server, MySQL, ORACLE, or some other variety?

What Information Do You Capture?

What customer or prospect information do you capture for marketing purposes? This question has two components. First, what data is your current system capable of capturing? Second, what data are you capturing? While you may have a database or system that can store every conceivable piece of information about a prospect, many businesses have not created the automation to capture detailed information. Some data, particularly private information, may be hard to acquire.

The purpose of this question is to establish the robustness of your database. Most commercial CRM systems come with an extensive database that include many tables, columns, and rows. So, even if you don't currently use all the tables, the fact that you have a full-bodied database capable of growing with your business is important.

CRM Website Integration

Is your CRM a separate application or is it an extension of your website? Is it a marketing tool or a sales tool? Do you have automated processes on your website, such as newsletter sign-up forms, landing page call-to-action forms, ecommerce, or other ways to capture customer/prospect data? Is that information stored in a CRM?

The same questions apply to social media channels. Are you capturing likes and shares from Facebook? When someone likes or shares, is their profile information captured by the web CRM? Are you tracking this information? While each social media channel is different, they all capture tons of data for marketers to analyze. Some commercial web CRMs already have the capability to capture social media data. If yours doesn't, all the major social media channels have developer environments for extracting data and populating your web CRM.

Customer Segmentation

Do you segment your customers and prospects into groups? For example, Facebook allows you to assign friends to groups. You can have business friends, family friends, and friends who aren't really friends. Then, when you create a post, you can exclude groups from being notified. In that way, you can directly post to some customers and not to others.

The question is – does your CRM system organize customers by groups? You'll want to know if you capture enough data about customers so that you can segment them into groups. Have you divided them into groups based on demographics, location, occupation, interest, purchases, and spending habits? What other descriptive segmentation makes sense for your business?

Prospect Scoring

Many sales and marketing organizations have gone to a formal process for rating a prospect's likelihood to buy. Scoring or rating a prospect's likelihood of purchasing was traditionally a sales function. The prospect is identified by sales, placed in the pipeline, and given a pipeline score. The further you move down the sales pipeline, the higher your score.

With the advent of the internet, prospect scoring has become a function of marketing as well as sales. When prospects visit your website, or interact with your social media, you can give them a score depending on what they do. For example, a prospect goes to a landing page that includes an offer for a white paper; free, after the prospect leaves behind a name and email address, of course. Once they give this information, they are graded using a point system. In the case of a downloaded white paper, they would receive a lot of points. If they received an email from one of your marketing campaigns and opened it, then they may receive a few points, but generally not many. On the other hand, if you lost an opportunity with a prospect, the prospect would have significant points taken away.

The question is: Do you score prospects manually, automatically, or not at all? Remember, this is a question for marketing, not sales. Sales organizations usually rank or score prospects, but marketing must find the prospects. Does marketing identify your business's prospects? To what extent is this process automated?

CRM Time and Resources

How much time, money, and resources do you spend on CRM? If you've purchased a CRM system from a software vendor, what did you pay for the system and are there any ongoing maintenance costs? Many organizations use a cloud or Software as a Service (SaaS) solution such as Salesforce.com. They charge approximately $50 a month per person for the basic service. Then, if you add other modules such as Facebook or email marketing, you will pay additional fees. What are the total ongoing costs?

Is someone from marketing or elsewhere responsible for supporting the CRM? How much time do they spend monthly to support the CRM? How much do you pay them? Do you hire outside software developers to build your CRM webforms? Fortunately, if you use a CRM such as salesforce.com, your $50 a month fee includes maintenance and support. If your marketing department is only three or four people, support costs are next to nothing. However, if you have a 100 people, you'll assign a couple of people to provide training and continuous assistance to those who need help, especially to new employees. Support becomes more expensive for larger companies that utilize enterprise CRMs. Generally, one or two technical people will provide internal support for the enterprise CRM provider.

In addition, quantify the time your business spends on supporting and using the CRM. We have found that many organizations have some form of a CRM and pay for it, but don't spend the time using it properly. We've also found other organizations manually collect and use marketing data from their websites and social media. While they have some CRM processes, very little is automated.

Conclusion

Every organization needs a way to keep contact information. It's how they can interact with their customers and prospects. Although this is sometimes a manual process for smaller organizations, as your company grows, so will the need for a CRM system. If we are building a foundation, a CRM is the concrete that holds it all together.

Chapter 5: Email

"It always seems impossible until it's done."
– Nelson Mandela

A few years ago, I was working for a technology company trying to break into the healthcare market. It was my job to find high-quality leads as fast as possible. I had good copy, custom images, and valuable technology. So, I bought a list of 10,000 names "guaranteed" 90 percent accurate. I spent the next few days studying spamming rules and best practices: I made sure to send out emails sporadically and never too many at a time; I created an unsubscribe button; I completely ignored the "don't buy lists" advice.

Out of the 10,000 emails sent out to "quality leads," 4,000 were rejected, a few hundred were marked as spam, and one lead returned with a call (they were quickly disqualified). Although the list was supposedly the target market I wanted, it was essentially worthless. It probably did harm to the brand.

Fast forward a few years to Impact Social. Although we didn't capture tens of thousands of names from the events, those we did capture were exponentially more valuable. Instead of a .01 percent response rate with zero other measurable metrics, we averaged an email open rate of 40.3 percent and a click-through of 2.7 percent. This rate was consistent within a few percentage points over three of the four markets that were targeted. The only difference between the two lists, besides the size, was the quality. We were able to automate data collection, segment prospects, and target audiences based on their interest. When it comes to email lists, the moral is: Cheap tricks don't work. Go for quality over quantity every time.

Email Channel Description

Email marketing is used to directly market to an audience via email. It has evolved from the early days of manually sending messages to your list. Today, email marketing is generally provided by online email service providers, such as MailChimp. They provide most of the automation tools required, except for the list of prospects.

Email marketing service providers track extensive analytics for each campaign. Information like open-rate, click-through rate, and purchase rate is invaluable for marketers. Marketers can also see how campaigns perform relative to each other and to industry averages. Email marketing can be used in coordination with other channels for increasing reach, traffic, sales, and awareness.

Description	Metric
Daily Emails Sent (Global)	269 billion
Email Users (Global)	4.3 billion
Email Users (U.S.)	245 million
Click-through rate (North America)	3.1%
Open Rate (North America)	34.1%
Unsubscribe Rate (Global)	0.127%
Email marketing expenditure (U.S.)	$2.07 billion
Average email ROI	122%

Table 5.1 Email Channel Description

Email Marketing

Email is a digital marketing tool as well as a marketing channel. Virtually every company that sells products or services to consumers use some form of email marketing. Our inboxes are constantly filled with advertisements, special offers, and last chance deals. So many in fact, that we generally delete or mark them as spam without reading. Yet, even though the number of people that open marketing emails have dropped from about 60 percent in 2000, it's still one of the most effective digital marketing tools at your disposal. On average, if you send out 100 emails advertising a product to your subscribers, about 23 will open the email and about 3 will actually act. In the marketing numbers game, this is a good result. We haven't found a channel that consistently produces this high of ROI.

If you have given your email address to any national retail chain or online store such as Amazon, Best Buy, Staples, or countless others, how often do you receive some sort of email? Several of then send multiple emails a day. For many of these companies, email is the biggest component of their digital marketing strategy. An email list that is well maintained and continuously scrubbed may be one of your business's most important assets. One of the challenges is keeping you email list up to date. People change jobs, email addresses, and positions all the time. So, keeping the list accurate, or scrubbed, is a challenge. There are companies, such as Siftrock, NeverBounce, and DataValidation that provide email scrubbing services that work with most ESP's. Many businesses still do this manually.

There are several email marketing automation activities, such as:

- Product Announcements

- Special Promotions

- Subscriber Newsletters

- New Member Drip Campaign

- Summary of Accounts Activities

- Change in Account Status

- Registration Confirmation

Many email marketing activities can and should be automated, like sending emails to new subscribers, sending account summary reports, and confirming registrations. Your job, as a marketing automation expert, is to identify every customer touch point to determine if an email should be sent, whether it is currently automated, or if it should be automated.

Email Service Provider

If you have a small- to medium-size business, you probably use an Email Service Provider (ESP) such as MailChimp, iContact, or Constant Contact. They provide services for managing bulk email marketing. In addition, they have the tools for managing email campaigns, as well as your subscriber list. They also track important statistics, such as email open rates and click-through rates.

One of the biggest fears of email marketers is becoming blacklisted or having their emails blocked for violating email spamming rules. ESPs are optimized for sending large quantities of emails, significantly reducing the likelihood of being blacklisted. Generally, web hosting companies, which host most websites, are not. It's ok to send emails to your subscribers automatically from your website to welcome a new subscriber or send a password change notification. However, if newsletters and bulk sales promotions are part of your marketing tactics, use an ESP.

So, the first question is "Are you using an ESP?" If not, then you probably have a very low level of email automation or email is not currently a major component of your digital marketing strategy. However, if you do use an ESP, then to what extent you are using email and what are your results?

ESPs such as MailChimp have several automation tools. MailChimp has automation as a top-level menu selection. Their website automation page has a variety of tools and email events you can track. For example, ecommerce marketers can track a customer's first purchase, an abandoned cart, who the best customers are, and what region they're from. Marketers who offer seminars and courses automate the onboarding of new students, deliver course materials, and follow up with students when they finish a course. In addition, there are specialized automation tools for nonprofits, software, list activities, music, and integration. How often do you email and which tools are you using?

Email Analytics

One of the most powerful features that ESPs offer is analytics. MailChimp keeps a comprehensive set of statistics for every email campaign. Your only requirement is to run the report and view the statistics. They track:

- Number of recipients
- Orders received
- Number of email opens
- Number of clicks
- Unsubscribes
- Bounces

ESPs also compare your campaign results with industry averages. As an example, Impact Social is careful about the names and email address that go into their subscriber list and they do a good job of keeping the list scrubbed. So, their email marketing campaigns that is designed to advertise events has a 40.3 percent open rate and a 2.7 percent click rate. This compares favorably with others in the same industry– 15.4 percent for opens and 1.5 percent for clicks, as reported by MailChimp. The significantly higher open and click rates can be attributed to a high quality, organically grown list, rather than clever subject lines. Do you monitor email statistics?

Cost and Resources

Undoubtedly, the single biggest cost in email marketing is building your subscriber list and keeping it scrubbed. Many businesses start by purchasing a list of names and email addresses. Generally, good lists are expensive and 30, 40, or even 50 percent of the email addresses are out of date. The best lists are built organically through a variety of methods, such as landing pages with a call to action, subscriber signup pages for newsletters, and online purchases that ask you to opt-in. Many marketing automation activities are designed to capture prospect contact information.

Other emailing costs comes from three areas: those associated with the email marketing service provider; cost of creating the email content; the cost of automating email task. The costs associated with the ESPs are generally monthly fee or a pay as you go plan. For example, MailChimp has a monthly plan that is free, providing you have 2,000 or fewer subscribers and send fewer than 12,000 emails a month. If you have over 2,000 subscribers, you'll pay a monthly fee that is tiered depending on the number of subscribers and sends. They also have a pay-as-you-go option for high-volume emailers. Most ESPs use similar models.

Non-ESP costs are associated with the time and resources required to develop the email content and manage the various campaigns. Out of all the cost associated with email marketing, the time and expertise required to create great content will be your highest.

Do you have a person(s) responsible for email marketing automation? They would be responsible for activities like creating email templates, developing software to segment subscribers, and reporting statistics.

Email marketing was one of the first tools available in the digital marketing ecosystem. Automation capabilities quickly grew as lists grew in size. It is still considered the best method of marketing for many companies, delivering the highest average ROI of the digital marketing channels. The first thing to do is set up an account with an Email Service Provider. This will help protect you from being blacklisted for spamming, keep your campaigns in order, and view the analytics on your campaigns. If you aren't using email marketing as one of your main marketing channels, it may be time to take a look at how MailChimp plays in the digital marketing ecosystem.

Chapter 6: Websites

"A computer once beat me at chess, but it was no match for me at kickboxing"
– Emo Philips, Comedian

Pizza Night

Around our house, Friday nights are pizza night. A few years ago, when our two youngest boys were in grammar school, one large pizza was enough. Discounts and special offers weren't that important considering we were only ordering one. Yet, those among us who have watched boys grow into teenagers know that eating like a bird is a temporary condition. Our boys have now reached the stage where they eat everything that doesn't move faster than they do. We're currently at three large pizzas and counting. So, discount coupons have taken on a whole new meaning.

There's one national pizza chain that is making quite a splash: Papa John's. In 2016, Papa John's sold $1.7 billion in pizzas. The interesting observation is not that they have grown to be the third largest pizza restaurant in the United States behind Pizza Hut and Dominos, but how they are doing it.

If you watch sports on TV, it's hard to miss Eli

Manning and John Schnatter, the CEO of Papa John's, advertisements. They take their connection to sports even further by linking their advertising to local sport franchises and celebrities as well. Here in Columbus, if the Columbus Blue Jackets score at least two goals or the Ohio State Buckeyes Football team wins, the next day Papa John's offers a 50% off coupon for all large pizzas. They got my attention.

But there's twist. When you try to use the 50 percent off coupon, you can't call your local shop and ask for the discount, you must order from their website. If you haven't ordered a pizza from Papa John's before, the first thing you do is fill out a personal profile. Sound familiar? Then, each time you want to take advantage of special offers, you must place your order on their website. We're trading discounts on pizza for personal information about us and our pizza buying habits. Now, three or four times a week we receive a promotional email with a discount code. It probably wouldn't surprise you that we receive a discount coupon every Friday, generally around mid-day.

Papa John's is a leader in digital marketing automation. Everything on their website is automated. They track who buys their pizzas, what kinds, how much, when, and which advertising campaign we respond to. Everything is automated from capturing your profile, taking your orders, sending you an order confirmation, and the advertisements you receive. As much as possible, they want their customers to place orders online. Armed with this data, they will continue to get smarter about their customers and how to customize their advertising.

Website Channel Description

Anyone reading this book will clearly understand websites. For consistency, we do provide this short description and notable statistics. Websites are a collection of web pages that can be found on the internet by a unique domain name. Though the quality of websites is as diverse as their creators, the one billion website threshold was crossed in September 2014.

Websites are used for shopping, emailing, blogging, sharing, posting, viewing, and just about anything. They have become so pervasive it's not unusual for people to have their own website for hosting their resume.

Companies promote their websites using Search Engine Optimization (SEO) tactics and paid advertising like Google AdWords. SEO optimizes a website to take advantage of Google's, Bing's, and Yahoo's search order algorithms that determine website ranking.

Description	Results
Total Internet Population	3.57 billion
Total Number of Websites	>1 billion
% of People by Age Group	
18-29	99%
30-49	96%
50-64	87%
65+	64%
Gender (as a % of the online population)	
Men	89%
Women	86%
% of People by Income Bracket	
$75,000+	98%
$50,000-$74,999	95%
$30,000-$49,999	90%
<$30,000	79%
% of Users by Education Level	

College Graduate	98%
Some College	94%
High School	81%
< High School	68%
Revenue	>2 trillion

Table 6.1 Website Channel Description

Website Flexibility

Whether your website is the focal point of your digital marketing strategy or not, all businesses must have one. It's the one place every prospect expects to find information about your business. Websites are the most flexible marketing platform to setup and offers the widest range of automation options. While it is by far the most flexible of all digital marketing platforms, it is also the most difficult to set up.

We say it's the most flexible because you control its design and level of automation. You control the products sold on the site, what information you capture, and what content each visitor sees. If you actively market on social media channels, you generally include links in those ads that direct viewers to your website. If you advertise products on other channels, you send prospects to the website where they can purchase the product. This is true for other activities as well, such as event promotions, white papers, and blog posts. Websites are where you turn prospects into customers.

This flexibility doesn't come without complications. For example, to start using Facebook, all you need to do is set up an account, fill out a profile, and add a couple pictures. In order to start using a website you not only supply the content, but you also create the site. This takes time, skill, and a little money. The flip side is that you can virtually automate every activity and customize the site to your specification. No other channel offers the same level of automation.

The best way to understand what can and should be automated is to perform an audit of your site. In this chapter, we review many of the primary tasks that can be automated. At the same time, you should review your site to determine how it compares. Therefore, in each of the sections below, we include questions to help in your review.

Website as a Marketing Channel

In Chapter 3, Marketing Profile, we ask the question "what is the purpose of your digital marketing?" Your website should reflect your overall digital marketing strategy. If you sell products on your website, mostly to existing customers, then your website should be easily navigated to find the item your prospects are looking for. It should also have a CRM that captures detailed buying and behavioral information about customers. If your business is a law firm, then it will probably look more like a brochure and have plenty of legal educational content. A video production company will populate its website with lots of videos showing off their work.

The purpose of your marketing not only dictates the design of your website, but how much automation is needed. Business that sell online will require more automation than simply setting up a blog for a sole user.

Automated Setup

After defining the purpose of the website, you need to identify what has been automated as well as what should be automated. Let's start with how the website was built. Most small- and medium-size businesses don't build their websites from scratch, but rather start with a website creation tool such as WordPress, Drupal, SquareSpace or Joomla. WordPress claims to run a third of all sites on the internet. These website creation tools have evolved to the point that they are now considered content management systems (CMS) because of their ability to manage blog posts, users, web pages, and other general content. So, if you don't have a marketing staff that includes HTML and JavaScript programmers, a CMS such as WordPress is the way to go. The point is, you don't need to be a programmer to build a great site. In addition, once the site is completed, these CMSs make it easy for non-technical people to manage. Managing websites can be very time consuming and a big expense. So, keep this in mind.

Below is a website automation table. The number of website infrastructure automation possibilities are almost endless. We have included a table that represent many of the popular website capabilities, page types, and plugins. The point of this table is to show the large number of options available for setting up a website. In future chapter on social media, you'll notice the setup options are far more limited. You may find you website infrastructure has features that are different from our list below.

Website Functions	Web Pages	Plugins
Purchased or Free Theme	Home	Administration
Post Comments	About Us	Affiliates
Facebook Likes	Services	Calendar
Event Management	FAQ	Categories
Event Calendar	Blog	Site Search
Ecommerce	News	Facebook Share
CRM	Contact	Widgets
CMS	Events	
Database	Products	
Ajax	Message Board	
SEO	Forum	
Site Security	Member	

	Profiles	
Page Security	Shopping Cart	
Social Media Links	Calendar	
	Landing Page	
	Login	
	Product Updates	

Table 6.2a, b, & c Website Infrastructure Tables

Purchased Themes

Did you purchase a website theme? Themes are a collection of web pages that are already assembles, having the same look and feel from page to page. You need to add the text, videos, and pictures. Professionally built themes not only look great, but you can generally find one that matches the purpose of your site. On top of that, they generally come with several built-in automation tools. For example, an event management theme usually come with the event management tools, some CRM capabilities, and ecommerce tools. Themes range in price from free to about $75. We've had good success purchasing themes from *Envato*, mostly because of their low prices and large selections. You can also find themes at *Themefuse*, *TemplateMonster*, and *WooThemes,* just to name a few.

Plugins

You then need to review what plugins you've installed. Plugins are software programs that can easily be "plugged in" to your site for additional functionality. This includes functions like ecommerce, event management, product portfolio management, form creation tools, web statistical analysis, calendars, and social media tools. If you use WordPress, plugins are listed on the menu under "plugins," of all places.

Web CRM

A web CRM is also a very important component of a website. Social media sites capture personal data about their users and sell marketing access back to you. With a CRM, you own that data. While it should be noted whether your website is integrated with a CRM system, the details of what to look for in the CRM is covered in Chapter 4, CRM.

Responsive

Is your website *responsive*? If your website is designed to display equally as well on desktop computers, tablets, and mobile devices, then it is considered "*responsive.*" Today, more than 50 percent of web connections come from smartphones. Some of our customers have over 80 percent of their website visits coming from mobile devices. Many organizations create their websites with mobile first in mind.

Automated Marketing

If you answered the question in Chapter 3 about the purpose of your marketing, you would have selected one or more strategies such as build reach, sales, and creating awareness, among others. Keep your answer to that question in mind as you review your site. If the strategy is to generate sales, what does your website do to generate sales? Do you use landing pages and call-to-action buttons?

What form of advertising or promotions do you use to draw prospects and customers to your site? This is the most important website-related marketing question. You are trying to understand how visitors find your site. Many of the website marketing questions you will ask in this section are a subset of "what are you doing to attract visitors?"

How important is content to your website? For some organizations, content creation is their most important advertising strategy. Some businesses may need to add content, such as blog posts, every day or even more frequently.

Does your website marketing depend on social media referrals? For example, Impact Social posts events on the business's Facebook page. The website has a plugin that monitors Facebook for changes to events and automatically updates the events on the website to stay consistent with Facebook.

SEO

One of the most important areas of website automation is Search Engine Optimization (SEO). SEO is exactly what it sounds like: optimizing your website to be the at the top of the results page when someone searches using keywords or phrases. Many tactics are used in SEO, like specific phrasing in website copy or linking to social media (called multi-channel optimization). However, the goal is the same: Get your website ranked number one in a Google search.

A comprehensive SEO audit could take several months, depending on the site. For our purposes though, you want to identify the depth to which you employ SEO and where your site ranks with your most important key word searches. If your site shows up first on the first page, you are doing a great job. However, if your site shows up on page 58 at the bottom, you are not spending enough time or effort on SEO. Identify who, if anyone, is responsible for SEO and their level of effort. Have you optimized each page on the site? Do you constantly monitor keyword search results? Keywords are the search words people enter on Google to find stuff. Is your site or page moving up in ranking? Your keyword search ranking should give you a good idea about your SEO effectiveness.

In order to work with SEO, it's helpful if you know a little about HTML. However, it's not a requirement, especially if you use a CMS like WordPress. They have a plethora of SEO plugins you can download for free. We have used the "*All In One SEO Pack*" with good success. It's easy to use and comprehensive. A simple search for SEO plugins should uncover lots more options.

Most marketing organizations have a target number for daily visitors. If you don't, make sure you set a target number for both visitors and page visits. We almost always recommend that our clients also set goals for search engine referrals and referring sites. These statistics are another good indicator of how well your SEO is working.

Google AdWords

Google AdWords is the most widely used of all website marketing automation tools. If you're SEO strategy isn't working fast enough, Google "*encourages*" you to pay for having your site listed on the first or second page of a keyword search. The more you pay, the higher your ranking. With AdWords, you select the keyword(s) you want your site or landing page to appear high in the search list. If you don't know which keyword(s) will generate the best results, Google will show you how many times users entered your specific search words over the past month and year. They also list additional suggestion for similar keyword(s) and how frequently they were entered.

Once you've selected your keyword(s), it's easy to setup a marketing campaign. You provide the keyword(s), the text you want to appear on the search results page, which geolocations you want the ad to appear in, and place a CPC bid. If your bid is lower than the average of others paying for the same keyword(s), your ad will appear lower in the search order. This may result in the ad appearing near the bottom of the first page or maybe not until the second or third page. If you out bid your competitors, your ad will appear at the top of the first page.

You can always try multiple keyword campaigns for A/B testing as well as test what happens when you raise or lower your CPC bids during the campaign. If you are not familiar with A/B testing, it refers to running different or competing ads for the same item to see which one does better. The good thing about AdWords is that you can pay to boost your site and drive more traffic. The bad thing is that everyone who searches using Google knows that those search results at the top and right-hand side of the page are paid ads.

The best way to learn Google AdWords is take a few dollars and do some testing. Like other target marketing tools, you will read about in this book, AdWords is mostly checking a few boxes and deciding how much to spend. You can set a daily campaign budget so that your ad stop when you reach your daily limit then resumes the following day.

Analytics

Do you monitor website analytics? Does your site track statistics such as:

- How many people visit the site each day, month, and year?

- How did they get to your site?

- What type of devices are they using to access your site?

- What location did they originate from?

- How many visit does each page get?

- What browser are they using?

- What search terms are they using to get to your site?

- How does your site rank with important search terms?

While this may seem like a lot to track, there are a boatload of free website plugins that capture all these statistics. By monitoring website statistics over time, Impact Social determined that most site visitors came through Facebook and that most of those came through mobile Facebook. Impact Social also tracked the effects of email marketing campaigns. Every time an email promotion was sent, the number of visitors to the website would significantly spike for about 12 to 24 hours after the email was sent. In this case, the website analytics started to paint a picture about the successes and failures of some of the marketing initiatives.

If you're using a website CMS such as WordPress, you'll need to install a site statistics plugin. WordPress doesn't provide statistics in its standard implementation. However, there are plenty of free analytics plugins which only takes a few minutes to install. Impact Social uses three website statistics plugins:

- **WP Statistics** is a free WordPress plugin that

tracks visitors, page visits, referring sites, and other site statistics.

- **SkyStats Pro** is a $50 plugin that tracks social media statistics from Facebook, Instagram, Twitter, and MailChimp.

- **Impact Social CRM Dashboard** is a custom dashboard that tracks customer and prospect events captured by the CRM.

There are many plugins that monitor website statistics, and most of them are free or can be purchased for $50 or less.

If you have an ecommerce or event management site, there are additional statistics you will want to monitor such as:

- Gross sales
- Net sales
- Orders placed
- Items purchased
- Discounts or Coupons

Good analytics packages monitor other statistics that may be of interest, including the IP addresses of visitors and search words visitors used to find your site. We've found that some statistics may not seem important at first, such as referring sites. However, buried in some of those statistics is some very valuable information. On one site, we could determine that 83 percent of their visitors came through mobile Facebook. This revelation resulted in a significant redesign of the website to make it more responsive for mobile devices, as well as modifications to their Facebook business page.

We've included an analytics automation list below. Rather than provide the names of third-party analytics software, we suggest analytics categories. If you are using a CMS, such as WordPress, they have a variety of plugins under each category.

- Site Dashboard
- Page Analytics
- Social Media Analytics
- CRM/Customer Analytics
- Ecommerce Statistics

Bots

Have you seen those annoying pop-ups on some websites that ask, "How can I help you, today?" Well, surprisingly, this isn't a human that just happened to sit down to their computer and notice you jumped on their site–it's a bot!

Bots are used for e-commerce, website navigation, RSVPing, customer data collection, customer service, and assistance with many website functions. They are already used by search engines and third-party organizations to track, index, and query your site. Soon they will be one of the main user interfaces for the digital world. Don't be surprised to see fully-functional personal assistants who know you better than yourself to be completely automated bots in the next few years. Think they won't be able to "run out," grab the meal you didn't even realize you were in the mood for, and have it delivered all with one button press? Think again and bet money on it. We are.

Website Cost & Resources

Many of the cost associated with building and maintaining a website are fairly easy to identify. If the site is hosted, how much do you pay the provider? Do you pay fees for ecommerce? Do you pay an outside services company to maintain your site? Do you pay for content, videos, or news? Do you use Google AdWords? How much budget do you allocate for AdWords? Most of these costs are easy to identify and, for the most part, not expensive.

The actual cost of running a website that draws heavy traffic may not be as obvious and is often hidden. In many cases, it's the content that draws visitors to sites. So, to keep visitors coming back, the content must continuously be added. Creating interesting content can be difficult and time consuming. Who creates your website content? How much do they cost? If you are a small business owner and the one managing the website, how much time do you spend managing the site and creating content?

The bottom line is, good websites that attract a lot of visitors are generally expensive and time consuming. Website hosting companies such as 1and1, GoDaddy, and Bluehost advertise that you can get your website built for a couple of hundred dollars or even free. While this is true, finding the best photos, videos, and creating interesting content takes time and marketing talent. And that's not free. In most cases, there is a direct correlation between the level of effort put into the site and the results achieved. Find out the real cost of your site.

Conclusion

The good thing about a website is that virtually every activity can be automated except for creating original content. Start with the purpose of your website, as well as the results you expect. Then, match the automated and less automated activities you found during the review against your website goals. The results will be clear as to what you need to improve.

Chapter 7: Facebook

"Man's mind, once stretched by a new idea, never regains its original dimensions"
– Oliver Wendell Holmes

The Candle Lab

Steve Weaver loves candles. More than most. In fact, he makes his living from them. Steve owns and operates The Candle Lab, a Columbus, Ohio company that makes and sells–you guessed it–candles! The Candle Lab offers candle-making courses, date nights, and unique scents. At $15 a candle, Steve not only has a quality product, but knows how to market it well. Steve knows his customers. He regularly updates them with new candle ideas and runs contests to see which candles are preferred by his customers. But the strongest candle market may not match up to what you'd first guess.

The Candle Lab scent library has an encyclopedia of smells you won't see in the Febreze aisle: Cannabis, Hops, and Wasabi are a few of the alternative perfumes. And they do WELL. In fact, the hops candle has an ROI 5-10x better than almost the entire collection! This isn't because traditional candle buyers love the smell of beer, it's a result of narrowing a target audience with the use of analytics, automation, and clever intuition.

Steve's first target audience for his Facebook ads was people who had liked the six most popular breweries known for their hop-heavy beer. He ran the ad. It did ok. It could have done better. So, who would like hops even more than hoppy beer people? Maybe people who went to beer festivals. Some of Steve's hop-head friends who were interested in the candle even traveled out of state to festivals. The next target audience were those who had checked into a beer festival in the last six months. He ran the ad. It did a little better! But it was still just ok.

Maybe hops just wasn't the seller Steve thought it would be. It was aggravating to try to guess at a market that just wasn't responding well and probably wasn't looking for candles in the first place. In a final effort, Steve was browsing around hop and brewer forums online and came across a thread. A few home brewers were discussing, with nostalgia, the smell during a brew. They were wondering if any of the other brewers had techniques for saturating their kitchen with the aroma of hops between batches of beer. Some boiled hop pellets, some bought essential oils, others had interesting ideas that didn't pan out. Steve had an alternative.

He posted in the online forum asking if his product is one they would be interested in, while humbly begging forgiveness for plugging himself. He found his target. Within 48 hours, he had 20 new customers.

In mid-2015, Steve plugged in his new target market, automated his Facebook ads, and gained insights into when his home-brewer market bought and who bought FOR home brewers. Steve also learned what seasons and months the ads did best in and further critiqued the demographics until the hop candle was the best performing ROI product. Without the insights, analytics, and automation, Steve would never have been able to see what marketing content was doing well.

He curated his content as well as anyone, but hit a plateau the first two times. The plateau was a result of the target audience not being quite right. Once he did find his target, he could use automation to get more and more precise with his timing, content, and investment. Eventually the ad plateaued at $0.60 per conversion (sale). At $15 a candle, well, you can do the math.

Facebook Channel Description

Facebook is the largest social media platform with 1.15 billion daily users. It's viewed as a socially based networking tool used to connect friends and family. It was founded by Mark Zuckerberg and his team at Harvard University and launched in February 2004. Initially the platform only supported profiles of Harvard students, but quickly expanded to include other Ivy League schools, followed by all colleges. By September 2006, creating a Facebook account became available to everyone 13 or older in countries with access to the platform.

Facebook has an expansive list of tools, options, and uses. However, the platform is typically used by people to share their lives, travels, opinions, and life moments (weddings, birthdays, etc.). Events, live videos, advertisements, and organizations are also an integral part of the platform.

The main part of the Facebook experience is the Newsfeed. This is where people keep up with new content such as events, status updates, and advertisements. Facebook's Newsfeed algorithms are designed to create the best user experiences on an individual level by selecting what content is most relative to the user based on their previous actions.

Because this is the largest social media platform, marketers, organizations, and corporations are a very large cog in the Facebook wheel. 50 million companies[v] spent $26.88 billion[vi] on Facebook advertising in 2016, an amount that continues to grow more every year.

Facebook is a publicly traded company on the

NASDAQ stock exchange and is worth approximately $390 billion as of early 2017, up from $104 billion on the IPO date of May 18, 2012[vii].

Description	Results
Total Facebook Users	1.86 billion
Daily Active Mobile Users	1.15 billion
Outside United States Users	86%
% of People with Profile by Age Group	
18-29	87%
30-49	73%
50-64	63%
65+	56%
% of FB Population by Gender	

Men	66%
Women	76%
% of People with Profile by Income Bracket	
$75,000+	72%
$50,000-$74,999	74%
$30,000-$49,999	69%
<$30,000	77%
% of Users by Education Level	
College Graduate	74%
Some College	71%
High School or Less	70%
Revenue	$27.6 Billion in 2016

Table 7.1 Facebook Channel Description

Facebook as a Marketing Channel

Facebook generates almost $27 billion a year in revenue, with most of it from advertising. They have over 1.8 billion users and 1.2 billion active users. In addition, Facebook tracks everything. Not just some things, everything–over 250 points of data including interests, geography, talked about issues, social life, demographic data, and which videos you watch. Facebook tracks and stores more user-centric social media data than any other social media platform. It's the platform you'll find just about every group you're looking to target. 74 percent of all Americans use the platform. In addition, there are plenty of automation tools for marketing and development tools for customizing your marketing.

Nevertheless, because of Facebook's popularity, there's plenty of competition for Newsfeed space from both advertising and organic content. Extending your reach to find new prospects with organic content is getting more difficult every passing day. Yet it's one of the social media channels that just about every business will want to advertise on.

Facebook Terminology

Because Facebook is the largest platform (in number of users and function), it claims the standard on most terminology. *Friends* are those you're connected with directly. *Followers* are those who are updated about your activity, but may not be friends. This is the case for people who have reached the limit of 5,000 friends (you can only follow, not request to be friends). Your *reach* is the number of users a post, update, or advertisement has "touched", not your entire network of followers. *Organic Reach* is how many people your post had the opportunity to touch (meaning it was in their Newsfeed or an advertisement they saw) without paying Facebook. *Paid Reach* is, well, paid for. Facebook's analytics are called *Insights*. Your personal wall on your profile page is called the *timeline*. You can add to *stories* throughout the day to update people with pictures and videos. This functionality is akin to Instagram Stories and Snapchat Stories. *Groups* are organizations on Facebook and can be private or public with various levels of restriction. *Pages* are generally organizational profiles, like companies or causes. *Business Manager* is the dashboard for businesses, marketers, and advertisers that use Facebook for paid operations.

Facebook Automation

Facebook automation capabilities are among the best of all social media channels. One of the oddities of Facebook is that businesses can't create a business page that is not connected to a personal profile. They have a Business Page, free automated marketing tools for various forms of advertising, and insights (analytics) software. There is more marketing flexibility built into the platform than any other social media channel.

In addition to the marketing tools provided by Facebook, there are a variety of third-party automation software options as well. The ones most people are familiar with are those used to manage content on multiple social media platforms. For example, HootSuite, Argyle, and Buffer allow you to schedule and publish updates.

If you or someone on your staff is a programmer, Facebook Developer has the most comprehensive suite of custom development tools of any social media platform. This includes nine different SDK's, Three API libraries, and eight platforms (iOS, Android, Messenger, etc.). Facebook provides the most flexibility of any social media channel for customizing your marketing.

Automated Setup

Facebook, like all other social media platforms, makes it easy to create business pages, add pictures, and post content. Similar to your website, you can create six different page types for Local Business, Business, Artist (band or public figure), Product, Entertainment, and Cause pages. You can also add sub-pages for Events, About, and Pictures all though you still need to come up with the content.

More than any other social media platform, Facebook has a variety of plugins that automate data and content sharing with your website. For example, if you allow comments on your website, Facebook has a comments plugin that allows viewers to sign in using their Facebook account. People can then choose to share their comments on Facebook with their friends. They also have website plugins for follows, likes, save, and share among others. Impact Social uses a Facebook Events plugin that syncs their website events with its Facebook page events.

While using the Facebook Developer Graph API and creating bots requires software programming skills, the rest of the infrastructure tools are already automated and easy to use. Facebook does a good job of explaining each of the automation tools. So, if you are not familiar with some of the tools above, go to the Facebook developer site.

For those first-time Facebook users that want a little help creating a professional-looking page, *Pagemodo* (http://www.pagemodo.com/) is designed to help create a Facebook presence. It offers sample cover photos, design tools, post design tools, as well as management tool. If this is your first time, you may want to give it a look.

Automated Marketing

Facebook has three basic marketing choices – content marketing, business page promotion, and ad marketing through the Business Manager. Content marketing on Facebook centers around creating a post and having it seen by followers. If the content resonates with your followers, meaning your post receives lots of likes and shares relative to your other posts, you may consider paying to have it *"boosted"* to be seen by a larger audience. From your business page, choose Insights and you will see a list of your recent posts and the statistics on how well they are performing. On the far right-hand side of each post row, you will see a *"Boost Post"* button. After you press the button, it will take you through several steps to select the geolocation you want to promote the post, the demographics you want to focus on, and your budget.

If you want to promote your Facebook business page, the process is similar to boosting a post. On the left-hand side of the page near the bottom is a "Advertise" button. Select "Advertise" and a menu pops up with several options such as "Promote Your Page," "Set Up an Ongoing Promotion," and "Promote Your Sign-Up Button." Select one of the options and you will be taken through an automated point and click routine of selecting geolocation, demographics, and budget as well.

Creating and promoting ads is somewhat different. Ads are handled through an automated marketing applications called Business Manager. It's set up to manage multiple ad campaigns and Pages in one location. You can set up multiple ad accounts and multiple campaigns under each account. You can also create multiple business pages and manage those pages through Business Manager as well. While you're responsible for creating the ad content and graphics, the process of selecting a target market and setting budgets are identical to boosting posts and pages.

All three option are automated and easy to use. The Business Manager, in particular, takes you through a series of steps starting with your marketing objectives (Brand Awareness, Traffic, Lead Generation, etc.). It's then followed with an extensive selection of "Audience" options for refining your targets. The marketing options are extensive, but totally automated and easy to use.

In addition to marketing automation provided by Facebook, there are many third-party tool as well. In Chapter 2, Eliminating Unproductive Marketing, we provided a list of the most well know third-party tools. Most, if not all, work with Facebook. There are other Facebook-specific tools as well. For example:

- **Post Planner** is a service used to find engaging content for various topics. It's designed to help marketers keep relevant content in front of their users and tailors posting time when users are most likely to be on Facebook.

- **Qwaya** is a professional ad tool for both Facebook and Instagram, providing a variety of functions for managing ads and ad campaigns.

- **Driftrock** is another professional ad tool for Facebook that is tailored to B2B. They refer to it as a CRM system for Facebook.

- **IceRocket** is a Facebook, Twitter, and blog tool for tracking mentions. You would use the tool to track when, where, and what is being said about your business or products. IceRocket claims to monitor over 200 million blogs.

Facebook has developed mobile apps to make specific functions more streamlined, as well. These are very useful if you use Facebook for more than cat pictures and Candy Crush.

- **Messenger** is Facebook's app that allows you to communicate with pages, people, and groups. Messenger's functionality will continue to expand by encouraging the use of chatbots for customer support.

- **Facebook Pages Manager** is the app that gives you quick and easy access to all of the pages you manage on Facebook.

- **Facebook Ads Manager** is an app that is streamlined for marketers using Facebook Ads for business.

- **Events from Facebook** is an app that lets you find out what events are going on nearby.

This is by no means a comprehensive list. A simple internet search will uncover lots more third-party tools. Some will be free and others, especially those tools that are monthly services, can cost upwards of $400 a month.

Before we leave Facebook automated marketing, there is another matter we need to mention. When it comes to marketing, the old saying goes "content is king." This has not changed! As a matter of fact, only the best content (as determined by the Facebook Newsfeed algorithm) is shown on their front page. This means that not only are you competing with other marketing campaigns for your audience, you're competing with their network for the top spot. Your audience must inherently want to see your message more than what's going on in their network, with metrics to back it up.

Remarketing

Facebook has the automation software that makes remarketing fairly easy. This is accomplished through a facility known as "Pixels." Remember, with remarketing, your goal is to identify prospects that come to your website or landing page, then advertise the products they showed interest in back to them. While it helps to know something about HTML, it's not required. Pixels lets you measure conversions, capture data to optimize ads, and create an audience for remarketing.[viii]

For remarketing, Pixels is a three-step process. The first step is to create a Pixel, which means selecting the Pixel button on your business page and having it assigned to an ad campaign. Once you set up the Pixel and associate it with an ad, Facebook produces a snippet of code. Copy this snippet and place it into the header on your website you want to track for remarketing. Then set up the desired "custom conversions" in Facebook Business Manager. That's it! For example, Impact Social recently set up a remarketing Pixel of The November Company to remarket wedding videography on Facebook. So, we created a wedding videographer landing page and placed the code snippet in the HTML header. The entire process took about three minutes from beginning to end.

Analytics

Facebook has a similar approach to automated analytics as they do to marketing. First, they call analytics *"Insights."* If you go to your business page, Insights will be a top line menu selection. Click on Insights and you will find all the statistics relating to your business page. There will be page likes, reach, page views, and a list of your recent post and their performance insights. The statistics for boosting posts can be found on the Insights page as well.

For ads managed through the business manager, just select one of your accounts listed on the business manager dashboard and you will find the relevant campaign insights. They include similar statistics plus cost per lead, lead clicks, and website purchases if you add Facebook tracking on your website, as well.

There is also a variety of free and paid third-party analytics tools. We have listed a few of the more popular ones below:

- **LikeAlyzer** is a free tool for analyzing any Facebook page. (http://likealyzer.com/)

- **Simply Measured** is an analytics tool that generated four different Insight reports. (http://simplymeasured.com/)

- **Agorapulse** is a tool for managing a pages

and content. However, they also have analytics tools for telling how well your content is performing and which metrics need attention.
(https://www.agorapulse.com/)

- **Scoreboardsocial** is a paid service that sends you a weekly email that includes page and post analytics and graphs.
(https://www.scoreboardsocial.com/)

This is just a small sample of free and paid third-party analytics tools.

Custom Development

As we describe earlier, Facebook has a very rich development environment for those who can program. Most of the 250 data items that Facebook monitors are made available to you. If you have a CRM system, you should be capturing Facebook insights. You can either write your own custom software or purchase third-party software.

While Facebook software development is beyond the scope of this book, it's worth going onto the developer.facebook.com site and looking over the documentation. If you are not a programmer, much of the material may not make sense. However, you will see the options and 250 insights that are available. If Facebook is one of your primary marketing channels, you may want to take a look at the Facebook Developer.

No other social media platform even compares with Facebook when it comes to advertising and automation tools. Currently, there are 60 million business pages and 9 million apps or websites integrated with Facebook. Out of the 60 million business pages, Facebook reports that approximately one million businesses advertise.

Rumblings

Like all digital marketing channels, Facebook has its curious idiosyncrasies, changing features, and helpful hints you should be aware of. We've listed a few below you may be interested in:

- Marketers, advertisers, event planners, B2B, and B2C businesses all pay to advertise products or grow their network reach. Why will they pay? It's quickly becoming the ONLY way to connect with some audiences. Organic reach, or the success your post without paying to boost, has been dramatically dropping since 2014 and will soon be zero (on publisher pages, it was down 57 percent in 2016). This is due to a few factors, the official one being cited as competition for Newsfeed placement has become much heavier as more advertisers are using the platform. Facebook's priority is always "user experience." With more ads, even targeted ones, the quality of the user experience will diminish which will result in a decline, or at least a deceleration, of active users. With competition becoming more prevalent for ad-space on Facebook, reaching the Newsfeed organically is approaching impossible. Every time the Newsfeed algorithm is tweaked for a better "user experience" the organic reach of pages diminishes. The new Facebook is pay-to-play.

- You can upload email addresses from MailChimp/CRM; Facebook Insights will give you information about those email addresses that match Facebook users.

- Hashtags help spread reach.

- Audience Insights ++: USA-based customers will give demographics about household size, income bracket, internet spending habits, type of vehicles driven.

- Buying followers is a questionable idea because it will skew who your true audience is, and the Facebook Newsfeed algorithm will rank your interest and engagement as "low," which will completely kill your reach.

- User-generated video has 10 percent more

reach than embedded (from YouTube) video.

Simple suggestions, such as remembering to include hashtags and uploading email addresses from your CRM or email service provider, can dramatically improve your marketing results with very little effort. Others, such as being aware that increasing your reach organically is becoming more difficult as competition for Newsfeed space intensifies, is good to know.

Bots

Being the largest social media platform, Facebook is also one of the largest hosts for bots. In 2012, Facebook claimed that 8.7 percent of its accounts were fake or bot-driven, totaling almost 80 million. Although a major purpose of bots is to automatically share, like, and follow posts and pages, a lot of less nefarious bots are adding value to customer relations.

Facebook has jumped onto the bot bandwagon with Facebook Messenger in a big way. They clearly understand that bots are already starting to play a significant role in marketing and expect it to grow even bigger. Recently, Facebook Messenger added support for *Chat extensions*, *Customer Matching*, and *Payment* bot development. They are also introducing the *Discovery Tab*, which looks to be similar to the iPhone app store where you can find Facebook bots and apps to download. As of this writing, Facebook has started promoting the Discovery Tab but has not yet made it available.

Facebook Messenger is filled with bots that interact with users who have followed you. At first glance, these turn Facebook Messenger into an additional mailing list; instead of a "lead," you have a "follower," but will soon be able to communicate with the full functionality of an Email Service Provider. Don't be surprised to see MailChimp and other ESPs integrated into Facebook messenger with templates, cross-platform functionality, and responsive bots. However, bots will do more than just provide message functionality. They can already find, book, and pay for travel; order food from your nearest Burger King; and give you data-driven diagnosis and health information. The possibilities are limitless.

Time and Resources

As with most social media platforms, Facebook consumes resources in four areas – the time and people required to create content; the direct cost of Facebook services, such as Business Manager; the cost of developing and/or purchasing apps; and the cost of advertising (and boosting post). Business pages are free on Facebook unless you purchase a professional Facebook theme from sites such as Envato.com, which generally cost less than $50.

The main cost for Facebook marketing generally comes from the time and resources needed to create content and to advertise it on the platform. Apps and plugins generally cost a few hundred dollars or less.

Your mission is to determine how much you spend boosting posts, creating content for ads, or spending per click. Facebook captures so many statistics from advertising and boosted posts that even if your costs are higher than your expected result, you will gain enormous insight about how to refine your campaign.

Conclusion

If you are a legitimate business, you must be on Facebook. Even if it's not your best marketing platform, at least create a Facebook business page and update it regularly. Many times, especially with smaller companies, a Facebook page will rank higher on an internet search than an actual website.

Facebook is also a double-edged sword. On one hand, there is so much competition to have posts seen that gaining viewers not on your friends list is getting difficult. On the other hand, Facebook has more users than any other social media channel.

The odds are, prospects in your target market are on Facebook. So, if you find that your great content is not getting the reach you need, paid advertising and boosting post may be worth the expense.

Chapter 8: Instagram

"Holding back technology to preserve broken business models is like allowing blacksmiths to veto the internal combustion engine in order to protect their horseshoes."
– Don Tapscott and Anthony D. Williams, Authors

Brick and mortar is dying and the internet killed it. Although this isn't true for every industry, many markets are closing up shop to open the door for ecommerce. Those in the fashion world know this better than anyone.

Kevin Black (@designerkevinblack) had a brick and mortar store in the Short North Arts District in Columbus, Ohio for two years (January 2014-January 2016). When physical locations were the only place to purchase designer collections, unique garments, and custom-made clothing, shop fronts did well for successful designers. However, due to online deals, focused searches, and a plethora of options, couch-based window shopping has started to dominate the fashion world. So, Kevin decided to grow with the fashion industry.

Enter Instagram: the most used social media platform in the fashion industry. In fact, 96 percent[ix] of fashion brands are active on Instagram, and Kevin is no exception. Although some business comes from word of mouth, about 70 percent is found through social media, with Instagram pushing 150 percent growth in brand awareness and sales revenue. It even connected him with Angela Simmons, who he has dressed and considers one of his biggest social media successes.

Kevin's use of artistic content on Instagram has even gotten him featured countless times on blogs such as Fashion Bomb Daily with over 1 million subscribers. He has used social media and Instagram to effectively reach clients and brand awareness. With under 900 posts and over 10,000 followers, Kevin is what many would consider "Insta-famous."

Instagram Channel Description

Instagram is one of the top five social media platforms with 600 million monthly users as of December 2016.[x] The platform is unique with a style that heavily favors visual messaging. Instagram was launched in 2010 by Kevin Systrom and acquired by Facebook for $1 billion in April 2012. At that time, Instagram had not reached 100 million users and was valued at $500 million.[xi]

Instagram has many of the same tools and insights that are found on Facebook. The main screen on mobile is the Newsfeed, where users view new, relevant posts from those they follow or those who advertise to them. Like Facebook, the platform's focus is on user experience. However, unlike

Facebook, this platform was originally designed for mobile phones (iPhone in 2010, Android in 2012). Many features, including uploading picture and video, are only available on the mobile site. This means most advertising, video capture, and picture uploading all use mobile-quality cameras.

Mobile marketing is Instagram's main source of revenue with almost 500,000 advertisers using Instagram as a channel as of September 2016. This is a result of the over 50 million[xii] (out of 75.4 million) millennial (ages 18-35) Instagram users in the United States alone. Although Facebook has not released any of Instagram's ad revenue numbers, Credit Suisse estimates Instagram will have $5.3 billion in sales in 2017.

Description	Results
Total Instagram Users[xiii]	600 million
Daily Active Users	400 million
Percentage of Online Adults that Use Instagram	32%
Outside United States Users	80%
% of People with Profile by Age Group	

18-29	59%
30-49	33%
50-64	18%
65+	8%
% of Instagram Users by Gender	
Men	26%
Women	38%
% of Users by Income Bracket	
$75,000+	31%
$50,000-$74,999	32%
$30,000-$49,999	32%
<$30,000	38%
% of Users by Education Level	
College Graduate	33%
Some College	37%
High School or Less	27%

Revenue	$3.2 Billion in 2016

Table 8.1 Instagram Channel Description

Instagram as a Marketing Channel

Instagram is the digital platform that took the phrase "A picture is worth 1000 words" to heart. The platform was developed for mobile use and is still primarily used on mobile devices since its creation in 2010.

Although Instagram is number three on the social media pervasiveness scale, it's first on user value, brand engagement, and product discovery. Users are 2.5 times more likely to click on ads, and their ads are 2.8 times more likely to be remembered than other social media platforms.[xiv] 60 percent of users have discovered new products on the platform. Instagram is truly the channel for visual marketers.

Out of 400 million monthly active users (more than 1 post), 25 percent live inside the US. This means 100 million Americans are using Instagram on a regular basis (compared to Facebook's 150 million Americans). This cannot be ignored by marketers. If □ of the United States is on a platform, you can almost guarantee some of them will be your targeted audience.

Instagram is best used for determining how your audience reacts to visual content. Although visual content is generally the most effective across all platforms, Instagram is built for (loosely) artistic visual content rather than a character limit or network enhancer. Like other platforms, campaigns must be curated specifically for Instagram. Similarly, Instagram posts never look quite right when cross-promoted over multiple platforms such as Facebook and Twitter.

Instagram Insights are similar to Facebook Insights since they are both owned and supported by Facebook. This means that much of the same demographic data and reaction statistics (reach, like, shares) is available. Similar ad categories are also available to reach marketing goals such as website clicks, audience growth, and product sales. However, Instagram has a few unique advertising methods such as "stories" that follow multiple chronological pictures and allow marketers to track when their audience "exits" a story. Be prepared to see "stories" come out on various other social media platforms in response.

Instagram Terminology

Terminology is the same as other social media with a few exceptions. A contact or friend is considered a *follower*, and you *follow* your contacts. Also, as with Facebook, analytics are called *insights*. So, throughout this chapter we will use the terms analytics and insights interchangeably. Other terms, such as likes, post, reach, and engagements have the same meaning as they have on other social media platforms.

Automated Setup

The first thing to remember about Instagram is that it is a smartphone-based app. If you don't have an Instagram account, download the app from the iPhone store or Google Play. If you already have an account, creating an Instagram business profile is simple–just click "Switch to Business Account." It can be found by clicking on Edit Profile. Then click the page you are an admin of that you'd like to connect. After you fill in basic business profile information, you're done. However, only the posts you create after you've set up the business account will be tracked for analytics. The real "setup" or effort involved in marketing on Instagram, is creating the visual content.

For those that don't have an Instagram account, create a Facebook profile first. Since Instagram is owned by Facebook, they share information. Instagram will retrieve your Facebook profile to populate your Instagram profile. You may need to write your bio and possibly change a few fields, but the setup is done. The setup is completely automated, but creating quality pictures and video, using relevant hashtags, and growing the brand's audience is what takes effort.

Automated Marketing

In 2012, Instagram was purchased by Facebook. While they are separate platforms, Instagram advertising is tightly linked with Facebook's marketing campaign manager. Before you can advertise on Instagram, you must first create a Facebook business page, establishing a Facebook business account. The benefit is that Facebook's advertising, insights, and analytics, is the most comprehensive of all social media channels.

To advertise on Instagram, go to business.instagram.com. On the front page, there is a red button in the middle that says, "Create Ad." Click that button and, interestingly enough, it takes you to Facebook's Ad Manager. Ad Manager is set up inside Facebook's Business Manager. The options are identical, automatically stepping you through a series of questions for determining the campaign's objective, geolocations, and targeted demographics. If you market on Facebook, Instagram will be very familiar. The only additional step is when you select "Ad Placement" (under Ad Sets, in Ad Manager), select "Edit Placements" and choose Instagram.

Instagram has four different ad types–Photo, Video, Carousel, and Dynamic Ads. The fourth ad type, Dynamic Ads, will be explained in the section on Remarketing. The advantage of ads in Instagram is that ads appear in the Newsfeed like other photos. Created right, ads can be almost indistinguishable from normal photos, making them more likely to be selected. Most ad types are fairly obvious, needing little explanation:

- **Photo Ads** are ads based on a single photo with a caption at the bottom. It will appear in the user's "Feed" just like any other photo. There are two things you should be aware of. First, Instagram has clear specification for the size, shape, and resolution of photos. Second, since Instagram is smartphone based, photos are uploaded and managed from your phone.

- **Video Ads** are ads based on video with an allowable 2,200 words for its caption. Similar to photo ads, video ads appear in the "Feed" just like photos do. Before you create a video, make sure to review Instagram's video specifications for formatting.

- **Carousel Ads** are ads that tell a story by using multiple photos and/or videos. There are restrictions on the number of photos and videos, but the specifications for photos and videos are the same as their ad types.

There are many free advertising options available on Instagram such as using hashtags, Instagram Suggested Users, geotags, and call-to-action buttons. In addition, there are quite a few third-party bots that can automate the acquisition of followers, add to your list of following, automatically like your follower's posts, and robotically generate comments. You can either purchase a bot or sign up for an Instagram automation service. Like most other social media channels, Instagram frowns upon the use of bots to grow your followers. They have started to restrict the number of users you can follow to 7,500. Remember, the quality of users you follow may have a direct impact on your marketing success. If you follow your best customers, you will know quickly how your products are received by your audience. You may also have a great source of user generated content (UGC) which can be an extremely effective marketing tool, just make sure to ask permission and give credit to all material that isn't created by your organization.

Instagram also has a variety of third-party automation tools that you may want to explore. Several popular ones include:

- **SocialRank** is an automation tool that provides insights on your follower's demographics. (https://socialrank.com/)

- **Crowdfire** is an app for managing your followers. It's a good tool for identifying users who don't follow you or are not active. (https://www.crowdfireapp.com/)

- **Foursixty** is an app used to sell products on Instagram. It provides a plethora of tools for building shoppable galleries online. (http://foursixty.com/)

- **Social Insights** is a marketing service focusing on Instagram analytics and marketing tools. Its emphasis is on growing your accounts, followers, interactions, and best times to post. (https://socialinsight.io/)

These are a few automation tools, but there are plenty more.

Remarketing

Instagram offers remarketing through Dynamic Ads. There are three components needed to create Dynamic Ads. First, is to create a product catalog through Instagram (actually Facebook). Then, setup a feed to each item in the catalog which includes images, product descriptions, and pricing information. Instagram does a good job of stepping you through the catalog setup process. Second, setup Facebook's Pixel for remarketing. Not surprisingly, Instagram uses Pixel as the underlying technology for tracking website visitors. To learn more about Pixels, go to Chapter 7: Facebook and review the section on Remarketing. Third, design an ad based on items in your catalog. The intent is to promote items from a product catalog across any device. You can run ads for hundreds of items to a targeted audience and automate the entire process.

The goal is to identify prospects who come to your website, then advertise the item they have shown interest in by "remarketing" back to them. Dynamic Ads let you measure conversions, capture data to optimize ads, and create an audience for remarketing[xv].

Analytics

The same analytic insights available from Facebook are available from Instagram. However, because Instagram was started as a mobile app, Instagram insights can be found on the mobile app, unlike Facebook (the Facebook Ads app must be downloaded). Insight analytics come from specific posts, stories, or advertising campaigns. As with Facebook, Instagram provides statistics such as impressions, reach, website clicks, and follower activity. For stories, they include replies and exits. If a viewer clicks an ad or likes it, we also capture their age, gender, and other demographic data.

To view insights from your post, go to your profile and select the image you would like to see insights from. Click on the arrow in the bottom right-hand corner. If you paid to have the post boosted, those insights will be separated into boosted and original posts. There, you will find statistics for Impressions, Reach, and Engagement, among others. Insights from stories are managed in the same way and kept for 14 days.

Ad insights are found in two locations. First, they can be found in Facebook's Ad Manager by selecting the specific ad. There you will find statistics for reach, results, cost, and budget. In addition, Facebook's Developer has an Ads Insights API where you can retrieve Instagram insights. This is important if you want to import Instagram insights into your CRM or analytics package.

Custom Development

Instagram does offer those with programming skills a development platform called Instagram Developer. The platform includes the Instagram API to customize the sharing of photos, creating marketing campaigns, and displaying photos on your website. Since Instagram is owned by Facebook, you can also use Facebook's developer environment to create marketing campaigns and extract insight data using the Marketing API.

Bots

Most Instagram bots are used to acquire followers, automate likes, shares, comments and follow posts to try and garner attention or a larger reach. Recently though, Instagram has clamped down on bot services companies in an effort to eliminate bots that automatically build your list of followers. In early 2017, the *Instagress* bot site was shut down at the request of Instagram. It appears as though Instagram is starting to get serious about eliminating "following" bots.

If you are trying to grow a following or need to gain insights about your audience, bots are the opposite of what you want. Bots work, as long as you don't get caught by Instagram for interacting with other accounts. In theory, they're used for repetitive tasks. They will like, comment, and follow those pictures that have the hashtags you select. But this is where it gets tricky. There is virtually no way to figure out the context of the hashtags you are following. The more generic the hashtag, the broader the content your bot searches for will be.

If you use bots, you will grow your number of followers, but they will be a worthless audience. Your audience will be inauthentic and unusable. You will not gain insights, know what is currently popular to your audience, and your home feed will be chaotic. Instagram has monitors that will trip if they see suspicious bot-like activity on accounts. This may get your brand or personal account deleted. It's probably not worth it in order to gain a lot of followers who won't match your target audience. However, if you are in a competition to gain the most followers in a time limit regardless of their demographics or if they are a spam account, bots can help you out! Instagram culture begets that your content, not cheap tricks, will get you noticed.

Rumblings

Like all digital marketing channels, Instagram has its quirks, changing features, and helpful hints we would like to share. We've listed a few below you may be interested in:

- Instagram has the highest engagement rate of all the major social media channels. Forrester Research found that Instagram users are 58 time more likely to engage with advertisers than on Facebook and 120 time more likely than Twitter. Over 70 percent of company brands will be active on Instagram by the end of 2017. This means that if your audience can't find you on Instagram, they may not even believe you exist!

- We recommended using hashtags to increase

your reach on Facebook. Even better, hashtags on Instagram are more likely to increase your reach than with Facebook. Also, there is no "astatic" limit on hashtags, more is better.[xvi]

- The Instagram Newsfeed is like Facebook's: the most relevant content will be shown to you.

- Instagram is heavy in "influencer marketing." This means companies pay users with the largest followings who represent their target demographics to sell products or services (lots of fashion).

- You can only follow 7500 accounts (to prevent bots and spammers from following everyone).

Simple suggestions such as remembering to include hashtags can dramatically improve your marketing results with very little effort.

Time and Resources

Being a free social media channel, Instagram's cost will generally come from two areas, paid advertising and the time spent creating content. If you advertise, how much do you spend on a monthly basis? Creating posts for Instagram consist of taking photos or videos and using photo enhancement software, such as Photoshop, to clean them up. Enhancing photos can be quite time consuming. How much time do you spend each month on creating Instagram posts?

There is other potential cost as well, such as monthly automation services used to increase followers, following, likes, and comments. These costs are minimal, generally on the order of $10 to $50 a month.

Conclusion

Instagram is unique platform that your company needs to have a presence on, especially if the product you sell is visually appealing or an experience. This means that all marketing should be focused around visual engagement whether it be pictures, video, or a story combining both. Even inspirational quotes should have an artistic or branded feel. Remember, you are competing with 400 million active amateur photographers.

Through the new business profile, instant insights and analytics are available to you that describe your target audience demographics, location, time of view, and responses. Trial and error, as with many digital marketing campaigns, will be the best way to gain valuable insights about your audience.

Instagram is the platform where quality really does outweigh quantity in a big way. If your post isn't up to visual par, it'll flop. However, if you're posting isn't consistent, don't fret. You will still have your space on the Instagram feed, free for your audience to see even if they haven't seen you in a few months. This isn't an excuse to be lazy. The time you aren't spending on posting needs to be spent on curating quality stellar visuals. No one got Insta-famous from posting reading material; looks really are everything.

Chapter 9: Twitter

"It is not the strongest of the species that survives, but the one most responsive to changes"
– Charles Darwin

Trump

No discussion about Twitter would be complete without mentioning Donald Trump, the 2016 presidential election, and the aftermath. Donald Trump lived on Twitter, tweeting early in the morning until late at night. Whatever was on his mind, he tweeted. His tweets seemed to have struck a nerve with his fans; they were retweeted twice that of Hillary Clinton's.

It's not the first time that a new technology changed the course of an American Presidential election. Back in 1932, Franklin Roosevelt was the first candidate to effectively use radio to get his campaign message out to the American people. He had to because the opposition owned most of the newspapers in the country. In 1960, John Kennedy used television to promote his campaign. Kennedy was a little-known senator from Massachusetts running against the older and more experienced Vice President, Richard Nixon. Yet on television, Kennedy appeared to be young, good looking, and charismatic. It didn't hurt that his father had been working in Hollywood for years and understood the importance of makeup and marketing. Nixon always appeared as though he had a five o'clock shadow, making him look somewhat sinister.

In 2008, Barack Obama legitimized the use of social media by raising millions of dollars in $10 increments. After, social media not only became a tool, but a necessity when running for political office. Twitter did more for the Trump campaign than most people may realize. For example, he would often use Twitter to test a message. If it resonated with his followers he would continue with the line of messaging in speeches. If they fell flat, he wouldn't. Twitter has the advantage of testing messages in real-time. He knew within hours, of even minutes, whether a message would work or not.

In addition, Trump's tweets were constantly being picked up by the press. Their analysis, both good and bad, gave Trump a great deal of free press. So much so, he spent less per vote than any other candidate.

Trump's use of Twitter has proven the power of social media as a marketing channel, especially for politicians. Clearly, he used social media to make an emotional connection with his fans, as well as enrage his opponents. So, as politicians prepare their next election campaign, expect them to become more proficient with Twitter. If you want to speak directly with your representatives, send them a tweet. You'll have a better chance of getting a reply.

Twitter Channel Description

Twitter is a microblogging channel for online news and social networking. Users communicate with each other by posting messages called "tweets" of up to 140 characters. The channel is predominantly used to send short messages about yourself or news, as well as responding to current events. It currently averages approximately 313 million monthly active users. As a channel for business marketing, Twitter represents one of the best social media channels for growing "followers" organically.

Other benefits of Twitter include its ability to directly message and follow any user on the platform. It's also one of the best channels for customer interaction, branding, and trending topics. Twitter is becoming notorious for its chatbots, estimating one out of every 10 users is a bot.

Twitter recently purchased two companies, both of which are video streaming social media platforms: Vine and Periscope. Both were purchased just before their official launches for $30 million and over $75 million, respectively. Vine has subsequently been discontinued by Twitter. Twitter is a publicly company with a market cap of $10.76 billion as of this writing. The company was founded in 2006 and is headquartered in San Francisco, CA.

Description	Results
Total Twitter Users	947 million
Monthly Active Users	313 million
% of Online Adults that Use Twitter	24%
Users Outside United States	79%
% of Users with Profiles by Age Group	
18-29	23%
30-49	31%
50-64	30%
65+	21%
% of Twitter Users by Gender	
Men	24%
Women	25%

% of Users in Income Bracket	
$75,000+	30%
$50,000-$74,999	28%
$30,000-$49,999	18%
<$30,000	23%
% of Users Within Education Level	
College Graduate	29%
Some College	25%
High School or Less	20%
Revenue	$2.53 Billion in 2016

Table 9.1 Twitter Channel Description

Twitter as a Marketing Channel

When it comes to social media, Twitter is one of the originals. Although Twitter hasn't grown as fast as other social media channels, it is far from dead with 313 million active monthly users (out of 947 million accounts). This accounts for 29.2 percent of all daily social media users. Approximately one quarter of them connect with a business and approximately one-third-receive direct advertisements and discounts on a regular basis.

As we stated earlier, one of Twitter's best features is a user's ability to directly tweet any other user on the platform. For example, if you're interested in digital marketing, you can follow the leading experts in the field, as well as start conversations and send tweets. No other social media platform provides this level of openness and the ability to build closer relationships.

There are other benefits from using Twitter as a marketing channel as well. Businesses use tweets to drive traffic to their websites, whether it's for purchasing products, reading blogs, sharing content, business news, or branding. One of the fastest growing business areas for Twitter is bots that provide customer support. If you don't have an active Twitter account, you could be losing a lot of your customer service opportunity. 77 percent of users feel more positive toward a company that responded to a tweet. In fact, over the last two years, customer service conversations on Twitter have increased by 250 percent.

Although the character limit is 140 (perfect for questions, quips, and quotes), Twitter allows pictures, videos, and links in posts, giving you limitless ability on what to post. Remember, the average Twitter user follows five businesses or brands. Are you one of them?

Twitter Terminology

Twitter doesn't have posts, they *"tweet."* Just like Facebook and Instagram, Twitter analytics are called *"insights."* When you share a tweet, it is referred to as a *"retweet."* A *"reply"* is when an @*username* starts the tweet and only goes to that user's feed or anyone who follows both sender and receiver. A *"mention"* is an @*username* that occurs after the start of the tweet. Your username on Twitter is your *handle.* All other terms such as likes, follow, and followers are the same as other platforms.

Twitter Automation

Twitter Automation is similar to most other social media platforms in that it has a fairly simple setup process. Automated advertising has many of the same options found on other channels and analytics are comprehensive, but with fewer data points. Where Twitter stands out is in its developer's platform, offering a variety of APIs and development languages. Below we cover the automation options in more detail.

Automated Setup

Building a presence on Twitter mainly consists of creating a profile. Compared to other social media channels, such as Facebook or LinkedIn, a Twitter profile is pretty simple. There are only a handful of questions to answer: your name, bio, address, and your birthday (if you don't mind giving out that sort of information). They don't distinguish between a personal profile and a business profile. If you've created a Twitter profile for your business, attach a great background picture as well as a good profile picture. Your profile bio is limited to 140 characters, the same as a tweet. Considering you have only a few words to describe your business, choose your words wisely.

Automated Marketing

Many believe that marketing on Twitter is about growing your followers list and for some, that may be true. However, there are a few points to keep in mind before you venture down that road. First, Twitter frowns on growing your followers list using automation tools. They have a policy that states "you may not use or develop any service that allows for the following or unfollowing of user accounts in a bulk or automated manner. Accounts and applications that engage in this practice will be suspended." Keep this in mind.

Second, several Twitter users with large followings have conducted trials that prove only 1-3 percent of their followers actually read their tweets. It's been found that one person can only effectively manage 150 followers, but the response rate and retweets for those followers are significantly higher.

So, be careful about purchasing that bot that automates following and unfollowing. Also, be careful about purchasing that bot that automatically likes or retweets. Twitter frowns upon that as well.

Twitter does provide a variety of marketing automation and analytics tools. For marketing, Twitter has four campaign types:

- **Click Campaign** is intended to drive prospects to your website by promoting, or boosting, your tweets to a targeted market.

- **Follower Campaign** is designed to promote your account by placing your business in the "who to follow panel." You only pay when a user becomes a follower.

- **Engagement Campaign** is designed to increase brand awareness by promoting your tweets to a targeted audience. You pay using the CPM method.

- **Apps Campaign** targets mobile Twitter users to install your mobile app. You pay for either the clicks or app downloads.

- Are you using any of these campaign tools? If so, what have your results been in terms of increasing followers?

- Twitter also has a large partnership network that has built some useful automation tools. Consider some of the following:

- **Buffer** is used to schedule tweets and RSS to send internet articles to followers.

- **Tweetdis** is a WordPress plugin for tweeting phrases and quotes from articles to your followers.

- **Triberr** is a community of bloggers that form group or "tribes" around specific topics. They retweet every article published by any member of the tribe to all other members.

- **Followerwonk** finds influencers by searching through bios for keywords.

- **Twitterfeed** attaches an RSS feed on a blog or website to your Twitter account. When a new blog is posted, it is automatically sent to your followers.

Twitter's marketing automation tools focus on driving connects and content between live users. While Twitter is probably the best platform for quickly growing your list of followers, they provide limited facility for capturing a follower's email. A big component of most organization's marketing strategy is to capture prospects names and email addresses for future marketing campaigns. Facebook and LinkedIn have facilities for gathering contact information for your CRM. Twitter forces you to use their platform to reach your followers.

Remarketing

Over the past several years, Twitter has used their website tag application to measure conversions on websites. In 2016, Twitter upgraded the website tag to what is called "*Tailored Audience Campaigns*" to better track conversions and remarketing efforts. Twitter says that "with the universal website tag, you can install a single snippet of code — the universal website tag — across your entire website by placing it in a global page header, on every page of your site, or in a third-party tag manager. Once installed, you can use the universal website tag to easily create and manage conversion events and tailored audiences without making any additional changes to tags on your website." The website tag application now works identically to Facebook's Pixel.

Let's say that Brian wants to know how many Twitter users are visiting his website and purchasing event tickets. He would install Twitter's website tag to track conversions and anyone that found the webpage by clicking a Twitter ad. In addition, he can use the website tag to create a tailored audience campaign that targets viewers that visited specific pages. Then, he can remarket to those Twitter users in future campaigns.

Bots

Most social media platforms have bots and provide a development environment for creating them. Twitter is no exception. In fact, the platform is quite conducive for using bots. The nature of tweets being limited to 140 characters reduces the complexity of creating a chatbot. While Twitter is trying to eliminate bots that increase followers and automatically like or retweet post, they do promote helpful bots that automate such activities as customer relations.

In the fall of 2016, Twitter introduced the new bot services "Welcome Messages" and "Quick Replies" focused on customer services. Studies indicate that when people use Twitter to seek customer support they want to get a reply straight away. The "Welcome Messages" are designed to directly respond to customer service request by telling them what they can expect to receive and when. "Quick Reply" lets the user know how to get their answer without human intervention. Twitter uses artificial intelligence and machine learning to better manage a user's interaction with customer service.

The 2016 US presidential certainly brought Twitter bots into prominence, where it was estimated by Politico that up to 80 percent of Donald Trump's Twitter traffic was generated by bots.

Analytics

Twitter offers several automated analytics tools such as Account Home, Twitter Activity Dashboard, and Audience Dashboard. Account Home contains the general statistics about your monthly tweeting. It also includes summary metrics on the number of tweets, impressions, profile visits, and new followers. The Twitter activity dashboard is where you find statistics about your individual tweets and includes impressions, retweets, likes, and replies. The Audience Insights dashboard is for information about your followers such as demographics, interest, lifestyle, and purchasing behavior.

Audience Insights are the statistics most used by marketers and is designed for Twitter target marketing. With Insights, you can discover the characteristics of those users interacting with your organic tweets. For example, if Brian wanted to promote one of his Impact Fashion events, he could use audience insights to find out the kinds of events his prospects have recently attended. Using this information, he can target his Twitter ads to the prospect segment most likely to be interested in his event.

Time and Resources

To be effective on Twitter, you must tweet. Moreover, to significantly increase your reach, you must tweet a lot. Twitter is one of those platforms that follow the old rule "you get what you give." The more time and effort you put into Twitter, the more likely you are to build your list of followers. However, this can also lead to Twitter managers spending a lot of time in the wrong areas. Though you may increase followers, are they your target audience? Is your target audience who you thought it was?

The two big expense areas for Twitter is the time spent on tweeting and advertising. It's not unusual for Twitter users to spend a couple of hours every day tweeting. So how much time do you spend tweeting and who tweets? Do you have a tweeting strategy?

If you advertise, how much do you spend on advertising? What Twitter campaign type do you use? What are the results? Your Campaign Dashboard and Audience Insights Dashboard will provide the data to easily answer these questions.

Have you purchased applications or plugins from Twitter partners? Have you built custom applications yourself? In many cases, partner applications are free or fairly inexpensive. If you're custom developing your own Twitter bots, the cost could be quite different.

Custom Development

Considering Twitter has over 40 million active bots, it's a safe bet to assume they have an extensive developer environment. They do. Twitter Developer has a wide range of APIs for connecting your website, smartphone, and marketing. For example, Fabric is a mobile platform that provides services for building apps. Twitter for Websites is a library of widgets, buttons, and client scripting tools. Cards is another app that is used to display content along with tweets for supporting links that feature photos, videos, and page summaries for shared links. These are just a few of the APIs and libraries available for building custom software.

They also support numerous development environments. By our count, Facebook supports nine different development languages. Twitter supports 15, including all the same ones as Facebook, as well as others such as Microsoft's .NET, Perl, and Object-C. If you're not a programmer, you may not care how many programming environments Twitter offers. However, if you determine Twitter is a channel you should be on, the large variety of development options means you are not restricted to one way of getting your custom code developed. It will be easier and less expensive if you have a choice.

Rumblings

Like all digital marketing channels, Twitter has a few interesting observations and benefits you should be aware of. We've listed a few below you may be interested in:

- Approximately one in 10 Twitter users is a bot.

- Twitter has a development environment, but does not allow for direct access to users' contact information and email addresses.

- After the 2016 presidential election, where bots played such an important role, Twitter tweaked their Newsfeed algorithm that distinguishes between bots and live accounts. Twitter now gives priority to live users over bots.

- If the first word of your tweet is an "@Username," then the tweet will ONLY appear to that user's timeline, not your audience's. To fix this, put any word as the first word, then call out to the users. "Hey,

@Username" will fix this problem. The reason for this problem is the fact that Twitter assumes when you are calling out someone in the first sentence, you are trying to contact them personally. This is why you will often see tweets start with a "." before the @username.

- Twitter's List feature can help you locate influencers by finding people who retweet, favorite, and reply the most often. You'll have a better idea about who you should target. This allows you to locate and work with crowd influencers.

- Twitter's Advanced Search feature will help you refine a search, allowing you to find your competitor's hashtags and customers. By using the geo-location and keyword search functions, you can narrow your parameters to the keywords that are important to you, or you can find potential customers in the city or country that you're interested in.

- Different tweets about the same subject tend to do better (with the 2nd or 3rd tweet having a bigger impact).

Conclusion

Although Twitter hasn't grown as quickly as some of the other social media channels, politicians and political pundits have embraced Twitter as their primary social media platform. It is the easiest way to instantly connect with constituents and respond to questions. If your business requires rapidly responding to followers or real-time communications with a large audience, Twitter is a great channel.

Where Twitter suffers, is in the time required to build your list of followers. You must Tweet regularly and there is no easy way to automate high quality tweeting. This requires time, actively tweeting daily, and continually monitoring campaign analytics to improve results. The most effective accounts are generally the most active and engaging ones. Following the data and statistics will tell you how your audience grows with different campaign strategies. What tweet is trending in your industry?

Chapter 10: LinkedIn

"Someone's sitting in the shade today because someone planted a tree a long time ago."
– Warren Buffett, Investor

Stay Smart

If you watched any TV over the past several years, you were bounded to have seen the Holiday Inn Express commercials where, after staying at a Holiday Inn Express the previous night, guests could perform amazing feats. For example, one commercial starts off in a nuclear reactor's control room where it appears the reactor is about to blow. Men in white shirts and ties looking like nuclear engineers are running around in a panic. One man is very cool, calm, and collected, giving out highly technical instructions. They worked and the *smart* man saved the day. After a big hug from one of the engineers, the smart man was asked by the engineer if he was new to the company. He responded "No. I'm just here with a tour group, but I did stay at a Holiday Inn Express last night."

The Holiday Inn Express *"Stay Smart"* commercials were intended to keep things light by using comedy. Holiday Inn's target market was business travelers between the ages of 25-44, a segment of the population that is heavily dominated by millennials. Their research found that that millennials consumed a vociferous amount of information daily, mostly on social media. So, Holiday Inn Express decided to take their TV campaign online to LinkedIn. They targeted sales and business consultants with their one-minute *"stay smart"* commercial, as well as created a Showcase Page. A Showcase page is an extension of a LinkedIn business page. They provide tips and tricks to travelers. Within 40 days, they grew from seven to 1,600 followers.[xvii]

Holiday Inn Express has grown from three hotels in 1991 to over 2,400 today.[xviii] They attribute a lot of their success to the *"stay smart"* campaign, boosting their online awareness by 8 percent and beat LinkedIn's engagement rate by 45 percent. To reach 25- to 44-year-old business travelers, they turned to social media, finding their market where it lives.

LinkedIn Channel Description

LinkedIn is a social media platform focused on business, employment, and professional networking. The company was launched in the spring of 2003 as a place for job seekers to post their resumes. Since then, it has grown into the world's largest professional networking site.

LinkedIn differs from other marketing channels

because of its focus on employee recruiting. By encouraging users to create profiles that look like resumes, the channel provides marketers with one of the best company directories in the market. Profiles are set up to include positon titles, skills, current company affiliation, and education. For B2B marketers, LinkedIn will be your top social media marketing channel.

On June 13, 2016, Microsoft announced plans to acquire LinkedIn for $26.2 billion. The acquisition was completed on December 8, 2016. The transaction resulted in the payment of approximately $26.4 billion in cash merger consideration.[xix]

Description	Results
Total LinkedIn Users	467 million
Active Users	109 million
Outside United States Users	70%
% of Users by Age Group	
18-29	23%
30-49	31%
50-64	30%

65+	21%
Gender (as a % of the online population)	
Men	28%
Women	27%
% of Users Within Income Bracket	
$75,000+	44%
$50,000-$74,999	31%
$30,000-$49,999	21%
<$30,000	15%
% of Users Within Education Level	
College Graduate	50%
Some College	22%
High School or Less	12%
Revenue	$3.2 Billion in 2016

Table 10.1 LinkedIn Channel Description

LinkedIn as a Marketing Channel

LinkedIn is the largest business-oriented social media site catering to business professionals. As of this writing, LinkedIn has over 465 million worldwide members. It has become such a popular site for recruiters and HR trying to fill jobs that it's generally the first place they start looking for candidates. Most of LinkedIn's income comes from advertising and selling services to recruiters and marketing professionals. If you are a business professional, you must have a profile on LinkedIn.

LinkedIn also encourages businesses to create business pages. If you are business that sells to other businesses (B2B), LinkedIn may be the best and most cost-effective marketing channel. Like other social media channels, they've segmented their members into hundreds of categories for marketing purposes. However, their categories differ slightly in that they focus on job titles, geography, companies, skills, interests, and other business employment categories.

LinkedIn Terminology

LinkedIn users create *profiles* like any other social media channels. However, instead of friends, there are *connections*. Your connections can *endorse* your skills listed on your profile; this means they agree and approve that you indeed have that skill. Users can also create *recommendations,* which are short paragraphs describing your professional strengths and skills in your profile.

One big component LinkedIn has that isn't found on other social media channels is the presence of *recruiters* who solicit users who may be interested in job openings. LinkedIn also provides the *Sales Navigator* for salespeople interested in creating new leads on the platform.

Automated Setup

LinkedIn's setup is automated and similar to other social media channels. To create a business presence on the channel requires you to setup a Company Page, which is not too dissimilar from Facebook's Business Page. The first order of business is to create a company profile, which consists of answering questions about the business. You'll then include a company disruption, add photos, your company logo, services, products, and links to your website. While you have a lot of flexibility in creating a company page, there are not a lot of automation option. If you have employees, get them to link their profiles to the company pages as well. As updates are added, your employees will receive updates as well. It also helps extend the reach of your company page.

In addition to Company Pages, you can set up Showcase Pages intended for promoting products or services. LinkedIn sets a limit of 10 showcase pages per company page. However, LinkedIn will extent this limit upon request.

The biggest difference between LinkedIn and other social media setups is that the Company Page follows the format of a typical resume. This makes sense, considering the channel started out as a site to post resumes.

We encourage businesses to create a LinkedIn profile because it's so widely used to find people and business services. If you are a B2B company, you must create a business page if you have not already done so.

Automated Marketing

LinkedIn has five categories of built-in marketing automation tools. They are:

- **Boosted Sponsored Content** allows you to pay to have your post seen by a larger audience. Similar to Facebook's *"Boost Post,"* LinkedIn provides the option to take posted articles and have them seen by a wider audience beyond your organic connections. This is a good strategy for businesses that focus on content marketing.

- **Sponsored InMail Marketing** sends content/promotions emails to targeted members. One of the biggest differences between LinkedIn and other social media channels is its in-platform email service used to communicate between members. LinkedIn has an automated marketing solution that allows marketers to send emails directly to other members. You select the target market and LinkedIn sends your targeted email.

- **Dynamic Ads** are customized ads. You choose your target market and customize your ad using content from the targets profile. What makes this advertising option different is its ability to personalize the ad. For example, you can display their picture or some piece of personal information on the ad while others will see their personal information on their ad.

- **Display Ads** are desktop display ads that are formatted for your computer rather than a mobile device. This is a traditional ad that appears on the target's home or company page. Fortunately, LinkedIn only allows two ads per page at a time, giving the advertiser maximum visibility. Links can be placed in the ad that send prospects to a company page, showcase page, or website. Ads can be paid for using either CPC or CPM options.

- **Text Ads** are like display ads, appearing on the prospect's home page or company page. The difference between the two types of ads is that text ads only link to the advertiser's website.

Like other social media channels, LinkedIn has third-party tools that can be used with the platform to automate tasks. However, LinkedIn does a great job of creating their own apps, plugins, and APIs. They make it easy for salespeople, recruiters, and marketers to streamline and automate their tasks. LinkedIn best practices caution against automation for scraping data and visiting profiles in bulk. In fact, LinkedIn has sued bot-users previously. We've listed a few of the software tools below.

- **Rapportive** is a tool that integrates LinkedIn connection information into Gmail at no cost. Rapportive was acquired by LinkedIn in 2012. (https://rapportive.com)

- **eLink Pro** is a tool that mass-visits profiles based on keyword search terms, finds their tweets and favorites them for you. The idea is to automate basic interaction so a potential connection notices you and takes action. LinkedIn and Twitter frown upon this method of connection. (https://elink-pro.com)

- **Crystal** is a tool that analyzes a LinkedIn profile in order to provide insight as to the connection's personality type. It then suggests how to communicate easier with the connection in question. (https://www.crystalknows.com)

- LinkedIn also has a suite of mobile apps (both free and premium) that make platform-supported tools much easier to use.

- **LinkedIn Job Search** is an app that helps streamline open positions listed on LinkedIn.

- **LinkedIn Lookup** is an app that lets you quickly find and connect with coworkers.

- **LinkedIn Learning** is an app that gives you access to education and courses from industry experts for business, tech, and creative skill sets.

- **LinkedIn SlideShare** is an app that gives you easy access to millions of presentations, infographics, and videos by industry leaders and professionals.

- **LinkedIn Groups** is an app that streamlines interaction with the groups you are a member of on LinkedIn.

- **LinkedIn Pulse** is an app that provides daily news curated to your interests and profession.

- **Premium Apps**

- **LinkedIn Recruiter** is an app that

streamlines the recruiting process by making it easy to review prospects, respond quickly, and stay organized.

- **LinkedIn Sales Navigator** is an app that keeps you connected and organized when using LinkedIn for sales prospecting.

- **LinkedIn Elevate** is an app that helps you share content such as articles, blogs, and infographics, as well as measures how successfully your content was received.

While LinkedIn doesn't have a plethora of options, they offer options not available on other channels, particularly the InMail marketing option.

Analytics

Analytics captured by LinkedIn are displayed on the Company Analytics Page and can be viewed by the company page administrator. Just click on the analytics tab. There you will find statistics for:

- Impressions
- Clicks
- Interactions
- Followers Acquired
- Engagement

- Total Followers
- Organic Followers
- Acquired Followers
- Demographics
- Trends
- How You Compare to Other Companies
- More

These statistics are available and updated continuously.

On the front of your business page, LinkedIn tracks four statistics: likes, comments, shares, and new followers. These illustrate how well your business profile is doing and are a good indicator of general LinkedIn growth. These statistics also let you know how well your business profile is being received. A growing number of followers is a good indication of success.

However, a better metric of marketing success would be to set goals for your marketing campaigns. Statistics such as interactions, engagements, clicks, and followers acquired indicate whether your marketing is gaining traction. For example, the statistic "interactions" is the number of times people have liked, commented on, or shared each update. "Engagements" include everything that "interactions" includes, plus clicks and new followers. These two statistics demonstrate the quality of your marketing by showing the number of people acting on your campaigns. We also recommend setting a reach goal for your marketing campaigns. The combination of reach, interactions, and engagements will be the analytics most frequently used to correct and improve your LinkedIn marketing.

LinkedIn Developer

LinkedIn, just like Instagram and Twitter, is fully automated. Other than building a company page, showcase pages, and creating content, there is very little left to do. However, LinkedIn does have LinkedIn Developers, which provides a developer's SDK (software development kit) for creating custom plugins. You can develop plugins for login, enabling LinkedIn members to login to websites using their LinkedIn profile, thus capturing detailed statistics about members that visit your page. If LinkedIn is one of your more important marketing channels, then capturing more detailed statistics and allowing visitors to log in to your website using their LinkedIn profile makes sense. Otherwise, LinkedIn already provides a plethora of analytics that help our monitor marketing activities.

Bots

LinkedIn is more guarded about bot use than other channels like Twitter and Facebook. Although LinkedIn does use their own bots to provide better functionality for users, it strongly discourages third-party bots that scrape for information on profiles and groups. They will shut down bots and possibly the accounts associated with them. Be careful.

However, LinkedIn is not anti-bot. In fact, they have started incorporating bot technology in the messaging system. Users can now have a "personal assistant"-style bot. When a user is looking at a new job in a new company, the bot will populate a list of connections who work at the new organization. If you don't have any friends who are employed there, the bot will give you a list of words to start the conversation and provide a link to the relative job posting. Once you've agreed to meet, the bot will check both Google Calendars in order to find a mutually suitable time to meet, schedule the event, and notify you about the meeting. Expect more functionality like this to assist LinkedIn users, recruiters, and marketers in the near future.

Reputable companies like Google use bots to scrape LinkedIn information in order to query and index the site. These are commonly called "whitelisted partners." LinkedIn has been known to file lawsuits against bot creators violating their terms and conditions. Our recommendation is to play nice and leave the bots to the whitelists and the Russians.

We expect Microsoft, the new owner of LinkedIn, to reverse LinkedIn's policy on bots in the near future. Microsoft is making investments in conversational and messaging platforms, particularly those with artificial intelligence. They see bots and chatbots as instrumental to the future of these platforms. In 2016, Microsoft purchased a startup call Wand Labs, a creator of artificial intelligent chatbots. We expect to find the Wand Lab technology to make its way into LinkedIn.

Cost & Resources

LinkedIn's basic membership is free. However, they do offer a professional membership that that ranges in price from $24.99 a month for those interested in promoting their career, up to $99.95 a month for recruiters and HR. The membership types are:

- Career
- Business
- Sales
- Hire

Business interested in marketing will tend to select the Sales membership, which as of this writing costs

$64.99 a month.

Other direct costs are for advertising and paying to boost posts. LinkedIn charges like other social media platforms, where you can choose to either pay by the click (CPC) or impression (CPM). If you are already advertising or boosting content on LinkedIn, you probably prefer one method over the other and have a good reason. Why?

The last cost area is page management and content development. How much time each month do you devote management and content? Who develops the content and what is their level of expertise? If you use LinkedIn at all, content development will probably be your biggest ongoing expense.

Conclusion

Out of all the social media platforms, LinkedIn is the best platform for B2B marketing. They provide several well-developed marketing tools to customize and segment your target audience. It may not be the first social media channel you think of when it comes to marketing. Yet LinkedIn is where you will find the best current information about who has what position within a company. People tend to keep their profiles up to date, which makes the list more accurate than others. In addition, considering LinkedIn was recently purchased by

Microsoft, expect it to become integrated with other applications such as Edge, Bing, and .Net.

Chapter 11: YouTube

"Content doesn't win. Optimized content wins."
– Li Evans, Search Marketing Guru

The Viral Pursuit

Nate DeMars, owner of Pursuit, an apparel store in Columbus, Ohio, achieved every video marketer's dream: going viral.

Pursuit has been creating videos since 2011. Most are promotional or advertisements with the overall goal of building brand authority and driving foot traffic to the brick and mortar store located in the Short North Arts District. Things got big when one of the videos titled "The 7 Things Every Guy Should Know About Suits" found its way to the front page of Reddit and received over 200,000 hits in a day. This led viewers to another video the Pursuit team uploaded, "How to Tie the Perfect Bowtie," which has grown steadily in views since December 2013 to over 3.7 million views as of February 2017.

The YouTube channel Pursuityourself boasts 8.5k subscribers and over 4.5 million views. More important than the number of views is how much of this translated to a return on the $2,000 investment Nate made to create the videos. None. Although the videos were educational, informative, well received, and well produced, most of the 4.5 million worldwide views were not in Columbus, Ohio. Nate had reached a huge market, just not the right one! Because Pursuit is a brick and mortar store, the success of the videos had no measurable effect on bow-tie sales. However, what these videos did help create brand authority. At least one person at every wedding Nate attends thanks him for his helpful bowtie instruction they saw that morning.

Nate's next angle for video marketing was to target the Columbus audience, those who would actually come to the brick and mortar store and recognize Pursuit as a community brand. Pursuit partnered with another local company, Hot Chicken Takeover known for their Nashville-style fried chicken, partnerships with the community, and philosophy of giving those who have overcome barriers to employment like homelessness, incarceration, or addiction a second chance. The Hot Chicken Takeover employees were measured, fitted, and suited up for whatever the next step in life may hold for them in the video "Hot Chicken Takeover: In Pursuit."

Though the video only reached about 30,000 viewers, the results were incredible, considering the audience was limited to the Columbus market. With the targeted local focus and community engagement, Nate has seen a year-over-year same-store sales growth of over 60%. In a quest of the right audience, Nate discovered that a well targeted

30,000 views will beat the pants off an ill-fitted 4.5 million. By spotlighting the passionate people in Pursuit suits, the brand shows there's much more behind every stitch than a thread count.

YouTube Channel Description

YouTube is a social media channel for sharing videos. Twitter users communicate via tweets, Facebook through posts, and YouTube through videos. In 2006, Google purchased YouTube for $1.65 billion, then integrated the platform with Google's AdWords, AdSense, and SEO.

YouTube's first video was uploaded on April 24, 2005. Platform popularity grew to one billion daily video views by October 9, 2009.[xx] The most popular video, as of February 2017, is Psy's Gangnam Style music video with 2.76 billion views.[xxi] By 2016, one third of all internet activity was viewing videos.

YouTube now competes with other video-hosting sites such as Vimeo, Instagram, Facebook Live, and Periscope. YouTube is still the most popular because of its pervasiveness and ability to deliver videos to almost any other media channel.

Description	Results
Unique Daily Viewers	30 million
Videos Watched Daily	5 Billion
% of US online users that view YouTube	81.2%
Outside United States Users	80%
Viewer Demographics by Age[xxii]	
18-24	11%
25-34	23%
35-44	26%
45-54	16%
50-64	8%
65+	3%
Unknown	14%
US Internet Users Ages 13-17	91%
Gender as a % of the YouTube Users	

Men	62%
Women	38%
Revenue[xxiii]	$4.28 billion

Table 11.1 YouTube Channel Description

YouTube as a Marketing Channel

YouTube needs no introduction. Like Facebook, it is so widely used for viewing videos that virtually everyone that regularly uses the internet has seen a YouTube video. It reaches more 18- to 49-year-olds than any cable network in the US.[xxiv]

When you sign up for Facebook, you create a personal profile and then a business page. To communicate with friends, you create a post and comment on friend's post. With YouTube, you sign up by creating a profile of your personal preferences. To share videos, you create your own channel and upload videos. People interested in your videos "subscribe" to your channel. For many years, TV was the only medium available to use videos for marketing. Then, only large businesses with deep pockets for advertising could afford to use video marketing. With the rise of YouTube, businesses of all sizes can create their own channel, leveling the playing field.

To understand the impact YouTube has on digital marketing, just look at some of these statistics:

- Over 3 billion videos are viewed every day

- YouTube is the second largest search engine

- It is estimated that 75 percent of internet traffic will be video in 2017

- It is 50 times easier to rank a video than an article on Google[xxv]

Videos rank so much higher than articles on Google because Google owns YouTube and profits from its use.

YouTube Terminology

YouTube is made of three groups: *Creators, advertisers, and viewers.* Creators create content on their personal *channels.* Channels are the equivalent to TV stations or channels. Creators upload videos to their channel, which are watched by *viewers.* Viewers are able to *like, dislike,* and *comment* on videos and channels (if commenting is enabled). When a channel starts to gain popularity, especially within a demographic, YouTube will enable advertisements on the channel and split the advertising revenue with the channel's creator and the platform. *Views* are the amount of times your video is viewed. YouTube analytics and dashboard are called *analytics* and *dashboard*. Videos are uploaded in the *video manager*. Past these, YouTube terminology is straightforward.

YouTube Automation

How are you using YouTube? Are you a video "creator" or an advertiser? You can be both. For example, ABC News is a video creator, using their channel for news distribution and current event stories. Their goal is to attract you to their channel with their news content. State Farm Insurance is an advertiser, paying to have advertisements attached to someone else's videos.

As a creator, you will go to YouTube's Creator Studio where you will find all the tools for managing your channel. This includes a dashboard, video manager, analytics, and video creation tools. For advertising, YouTube offers many automated advertising tools such as TrueView In-stream ads and display ads among others. You'll find a list of the advertising tools on the footer menu item "advertise."

YouTube is one of the platforms in which consistently updating and creating content is very important. Re-runs still aren't as popular as new content. However, what content works best is determined by studying Google Analytics and

TrueView, the tools YouTube uses to measure marketing success.

Automated Setup

There is not much to automate when it comes to creating a YouTube channel. Upon signing up for YouTube, you create a profile. The profile has the same generic information other social media channels have, such as name, age, email, phone, etc. Your YouTube site will have a Homepage, which lists video from the channels you subscribe to (follow), an advertisement banner at the top of the page, and a menu bar on the left-hand side.

The My Channel page is where your videos are located. Other than the videos you create and upload, make sure you fill in the channel description. Google uses the tags and keywords in the description to find your channel. So, use the same SEO techniques you would when creating a web page. The real effort is not in setting up the channel but in creating videos. Virtually everything else is automated.

Automated Marketing

Creators and advertisers are both marketers, but

generally with two different goals. However, they both work together with the YouTube platform in the same way cable and radio always have: through commercials. With TrueView and YouTube Analytics, both Advertisers and Creators can test, promote, and pivot their content depending on audience response.

There are multiple automated YouTube advertising tools. The most dominant are the in-stream advertising and the in-display advertising. In-stream advertisements are those that appear prior to your selected video running. After five seconds, the viewer can skip the advertisement and go directly to the video or they can continue watching the whole thing. An in-display ad appears to the right of the featured video.

There are several advertising modes to choose from:

- **TrueView in-stream ads** are ads that appear prior to the actual video starting. After the ad has played for 5 seconds, the viewer can continue watching or skip the ad. If they continue watching the ad for at least 30 seconds, the advertiser will be charged. There is a "non-skippable" ad version as well, but this will be going away in 2018.

- **TrueView Video Discovery** are ads that appear alongside your video on the right-hand side of the page. You only pay when the user clicks on the ad.

- **Standard Display Ads** is an ad that can appear on any YouTube page, with the exception of the home page. They have a standard size 300x250 display format.

- **In-Video Overlay Ads** are 470x80 ads that appear at the bottom of a video. It looks like a banner.

- **Mastheads** – are videos that run silently until they are clicked and play on the YouTube homepage, like an online billboard. The advertisement is purchased for a full day, running from 12:00 AM local time until 11:59 PM. There are three types of Mastheads:
  - Desktop
  - Mobile
  - Rich Media

While we mention Mastheads, be aware that the cost is generally in the hundreds of thousands of dollars. When one marketer made an inquiry with YouTube about the price of Mastheads, the response was "if you don't have a Google sales rep, you can't afford it." They're not cheap.

TrueView ads are those that can be skipped after five seconds. YouTube has several options for placing ads in-stream, in-search, in-state, and in-display. A Masthead ad is a video that run on the desktop or mobile phone silently until it is clicked. Marketers pay for the ads in 24 hour increments, not by the click.

Remarketing

When we think of remarketing, YouTube is generally not the first marketing channel that comes to mind. However, YouTube offers very advanced remarketing automation. Remarketing is done through Google AdWords, giving you the ability to remarket to those that have viewed your video or YouTube channel. You can create marketing list of viewers that have done any of the following:

- Viewed a video from your channel

- Visited a channel page

- Viewed any video (as an ad) from a channel

- Liked any video from a channel

- Commented on any video from a channel

- Shared any video from a channel

- Subscribed to a channel

- Viewed certain video(s)

- Viewed certain video(s) as ad(s)[xxvi]

Remarketing with Google AdWords works

differently than Facebook's Pixel. Google uses a special tracking code to place cookies on the computers of those who view your video. The cookies can then be used to remarket from YouTube and on the web using Google Display Network as well. Google Display Network is a component of AdWords.

Analytics

The most important statistic to follow is "Watch Time." If viewers are only watching 10 seconds of a two-minute video, then there is probably an issue with the video. If viewers watch it to the end or at least to the point where you ask them to act, then it is probably an interesting video. As a marketer, this one statistic tells you a lot about how your video marketing is being received.

Other statistics are important as well, such as views, likes, comments, shares, and subscribers. YouTube has an excellent analytics page that describes how well each video is doing. In addition to the above statistics, they provide gender, traffic source, and geographic location.

Finding standard YouTube analytics is not as obvious as it is with other social media platforms. You need to do a little searching. First, find the account icon in the upper right-hand corner of your home page. When you select the account icon, you will see Creator Studio button. Selecting this button will take you to YouTube analytics. The first page will be a dashboard that includes your recent videos with their viewing statistics. In addition, on the left-hand side of the page is a menu with analytics as one of the selections. There you will find just about every conceivable statistic relating to your video channel, including watch time report, demographics, traffic source, and many others. Most of the statistics focus on your channel's performance, but individual video statistics are there as well.

As you investigate YouTube as a marketing channel, you will notice most of the automation tools are built by Google. For statistics, Google Analytics (or AdWords) can be used to monitor advertising on your YouTube channel and your website. Google Analytics provides statistics on visitors, clicks, discussions, videos, and playlist. However, detailed video statistics will still come from YouTube. If you're familiar with Google Analytics for your website, setting it up for your YouTube Channel is very similar.

Because YouTube is tightly integrated with Google, especially Google Analytics and AdWords, there are many third-party dashboards available for tracking marketing analytics.

YouTube Developer

Another less popular method for capturing analytics is YouTube Developer. Like other social media channels, YouTube offers a set of APIs' using HTTPS and provides sample code snippet examples. While it helps to be a programmer, the instructions they provide are excellent and modifying the samples they provide is not difficult. So, if you are adventurous, give it a shot.

There are four APIs – Data, Live Streaming, Analytics, and Client Libraries. To import analytics data to your CRM, use the Analytics API. It provides video details such as likes, shares, click-through-rate, close-rate, and watch time. They also track every video-related statistic: your channel's playlist, engagement metrics, view metrics, and watch time metrics. While you can use the YouTube Developer to automate a variety of tasks, capturing analytics is its most prevalent activity.

Bots

While some marketing channels encourage bots or at least don't restrict them, YouTube is not one of them. They frown upon bots and discourage their use. Bots are used to increase video likes, subscribers, favorites, and comments. However, inflating video likes is a problem because YouTube has a partnership program where they pay partners by the number of views. So, artificially inflating the view numbers of a big problem for YouTube. If YouTube feels your channel metrics are being inflated by bots, they will shut your channel down. However, third-parties continue to sell bots and bot services.

Time and Resources

The biggest expense with YouTube is generally associated with creating videos. If you are running around with your iPhone creating user generated videos and quickly uploading them to YouTube, your cost may be minimal. However, professionally produced videos can be expensive. For most, creating the video is the most expensive component of YouTube marketing. Are your videos created in-house or by an outside agency? What do the video cost to create? What's your budget?

In addition, if you advertise, what is your budget? Who manages your YouTube marketing, and how much time do they spend monthly? There can be other expenses as well, such as third-party analytics software, but generally these costs are small compared to the time and expense of create videos.

Rumblings

YouTube is a highly visible and well known channel that doesn't have a lot of secrets to be aware of. We've listed a couple below:

- YouTube announced they were getting rid of "non-skippable" ads by 2018. Those are the ones you can't skip after 5 seconds. Good.

- Google rates videos higher on web searches than posts, meaning that your video could easily rank higher on a Google keyword search than your website.

- YouTube Red gives you access to YouTube without the ads ($10/month). It also offers original shows, offline viewing, and continuous audio when you turn a screen off (a very big annoyance for mobile viewers).

- YouTube TV (tv.youtube.com) lets you stream ABC, CBS, FOX, NBC, and more ($35/month). They, just like other social media platforms, recognize that cable TV is on the decline. Younger viewers are finding more and more of their video entertainment over the internet.

- YouTube reserves the right to pull ads from creators and videos at any time, essentially cutting off their revenue. Their guidelines states that "nudity or sexual content, harmful or dangerous content, violent or graphic content, copyrighted material, and hateful content" won't be tolerated. These guidelines are left up to moderators to determine if a guideline has been crossed and have caused controversies in the past.

Remember, bots are very much frowned upon by YouTube and could get you booted off.

From time to time, YouTube does experience problems playing videos. However, most of those appear to be related to the use of older browsers.

Conclusion

While YouTube marketing automation tools are not numerous, they do have a number of excellent options for customizing advertising and generating analytics. In addition, YouTube is owned by Google. Thus, they provide video creators the same SEO options you would find for marketing websites.

YouTube will not be the platform for every business. Yet most businesses will benefit from having a presence on YouTube. One reason for encouraging businesses to build a marketing presence on YouTube is that more and more people are moving away from traditional TV to online videos for entertainment, news, and education. In

2017, Barron's expects digital ads to overtake TV ads for the first time.[xxvii] Together, Google and Facebook will account for 54 percent of all digital advertising. Don't be surprised if YouTube becomes the primary social media marketing channel.

Chapter 12: The New Marketing Ecosystem

"People who are crazy enough to believe they can change the world are to ones who do."
– Steve Jobs, Apple Co-founder

Moore's Law

Now that marketing has entered the digital age, Moore's Law will apply to marketing automation as well. If you have never heard of Moore's Law, it was an observation made by Gordon Moore, one of the founders of Intel Corporation. Back in the late 60s, Dr. Moore noticed that the number of transistors in an integrated circuit double about every eighteen months. In fact, the law has held true for the past 50 years and has come to define an entire computer industry.

Marketing automation has been placed on that same track. What was state-of-the-art technology two years ago is now considered old news. As soon as you implement the newest technology, it will not be very long before you look for the next upgrade. Those with the financial wherewithal to keep up to date will have an enormous edge in marketing.

Current State of Marketing Automation

If we were discussing marketing automation 12 to 15 years ago, the conversation would be centered around email marketing. Five to 10 years ago, the conversation would have included web CRMs. They were a big leap forward for marketing automation. CRMs made it possible to capture customer and prospect data when they visited our websites. Initially, we weren't as concerned about tracking prospect behavior as we were about getting their name and email addresses so we could include them on our email marketing list. As CRMs became more sophisticated, we started capturing other prospect information such as the pages they visited, the events they signed up to attend, and the products they purchased. We were becoming more knowledgeable about our prospects and which ones were most likely to buy. More than anything, we could identify who not to market to.

The most significant automation tipping point came in 2007 with the near simultaneous introduction of smartphones and the rise of social media. Almost instantly, both had profound effects on how we communicate with each other, how we spend our free time, and where we get our news. Social media adopted the same business model used by public TV and radio, their services were free to users while supporting themselves through business advertising. As users, we may view Facebook as a way to stay in contact with our friends. As a business, Facebook sees itself as an advertising platform. Their path to higher revenue depends on having a large user base, knowing as much as possible about their users, and making it easy for their business customers to advertise to those users. That's why every social media platform has gone the extra mile to automate their marketing tools. High-precision target marketing is now little more than a series of clicks and checkboxes.

The tipping point that started around 2007 also changed marketing in other ways as well. Up to that point, web marketing was centered around the company's website. Suddenly, there were other channels to focus on as well. Rather than having one place to manage prospect information, we had dozens. We needed to capture data from multiple channels and find a way to use that data to create an image of our customers and our business. Managing data from our websites, Facebook, LinkedIn, Twitter, YouTube, and Google Analytics requires wide-ranging automation, but it's proven to be well worth the effort.

The second element of the 2007 tipping point was the introduction of smartphones. It's easy for us to think of smartphones as just a new communications channel, but they are a marketing channel as well. Earlier in this book, we reported that one of our customers noticed 82 percent of their prospects originated from Facebook. Of that 82 percent, 80 percent came from the Facebook mobile app. Knowing that approximately 70 percent of their visitors use mobile Facebook was invaluable in terms of knowing how viewers found them, as well as how to format advertising and where to advertise.

Social media platforms have grown so quickly as marketing platforms in part because they capture data on everything. Facebook maintains over 250 individual data points and provides comprehensive analytics about users, demographics, and trends. Every social media platform has several automated analytics dashboards for monitoring campaign results. They also provide development environments for custom automation and deeper digging analytics. These development environments will become increasingly important as CRMs become the central repository for all marketing data.

The fact is, we already have the technology to automate every aspect of marketing. Bots have already started to automate every marketing task, like growing your list of followers, liking post with hashtags you monitor, and conversing with other users. However, businesses run the gambit in their approach to automation. Some businesses, such as Amazon and Google, have automated everything, while other businesses have automated virtually nothing. Smaller businesses generally fall into this second category. Yet, once these small businesses do decide to take an automation approach to marketing, the results are always worth the effort, if executed properly.

Marketing has entered a new era where automation, especially software, is as important as creativity and consumer psychology. Automation is giving us the ability to do high precision target marketing as well as track every click, page view, and site visit. Yet even with the extensive number of automation tools available to marketers, most businesses treat digital marketing channels as silos, sharing very little information.

The Next Two to Five Years

Over the next several years, marketing will continue to evolve from a series of standalone marketing channels into a connected ecosystem. Your website, Facebook, LinkedIn, Twitter, and mobile apps will form a network where each channel communicates with your CRM, ultimately tracking prospects and user behavior as they move around the internet. Thus, CRMs will continue to grow in importance, becoming the central marketing repository and data aggregator. The difference will be that far more data will come from other sources, such as social media, not just websites.

There are other technologies that will become more prevalent as well. Artificial Intelligence and predictive software are among them. Look for the following technologies to emerge over the next few years.

Artificial Intelligence

Businesses are already using artificial intelligence in a number of different ways. Chatbots with AI already carry on remedial conversations with other users; we touched on some of them when we reviewed Twitter. Customer support organizations are also starting to use chatbots to address the most common customer questions. This is big time saver for many support organizations, considering up to 70 percent of customer inquiries are repetitive. Because of their growth, businesses are already starting to drop their (800) numbers in favor of chatbots. Intelligent bots are taking a significant burden off customer support.

Social media platforms have already started moving aggressively to incorporate AI into all aspects of their platforms. For example, Facebook has made a serious commitment to AI, with its investment in Facebook Artificial Intelligence Research (FAIR) group. FAIR's mission is to "understand and develop systems with human level intelligence." The company already has 40 team members and 25 percent of their engineers using AI to build software products[xxviii]. In 2015, Twitter purchased a five-person artificial intelligence startup called Whetlab in order to upgrade artificial intelligence capabilities. Other social media companies are actively building their AI capabilities as well.

Web Scraping

Web *scraping* refers to an automated process that uses bots or web crawlers to extract (scrape) data from websites. Essentially, a web page is downloaded and the content of the page is parsed, looking for specific words or phrases. Web crawlers and bots have been used since the invention of the internet by search engines to gather keyword ranking data. Now we're starting to see scraping technology used in marketing for a variety of activities. For example, we work with a company that has scraping software that was used in the 2016 Ohio Senatorial election to identify voters from several counties that were concerned about the recent rise in drug-related deaths. Once the voters were identified, the candidate created a remarketing campaign to sway those voters. In addition, we used similar scraping software to identify sales prospects.

While scraping is already a widely-used technology by search engines, it is only beginning to take center stage in marketing. Expect scraping products to identify sales prospects, monitor customer sentiment, and identify real-time changes in market direction to emerge over the next couple of years.

Predictive Marketing

For the most part, marketing analytics are collected and then summarized on dashboards and social media insight pages. Then, with our experience and intuition as marketers, we review the data and make the appropriate marketing adjustments. While the collection of data is automated, the analysis is manual. Predictive marketing will take analytics technology one step further, adding artificial intelligence that makes educated predictions based on historical data and trend analysis. You already see this technology being used by Amazon Kindle presenting books they think you might like to read and Netflix offering new movies you might like to watch.

Predictive analytics will become more frequently used in a variety of marketing areas such as sales forecasting, estimating demand, and predicting trends. It not only uses the data you capture, but also includes larger data sets that are publicly available. This enables the predictive software to include other data you may not possess, such as competitor's information, market trends, and other historical data.

Big Brother

In 1949, George Orwell published the dystopian novel *1984*. In it, he described a totalitarian society where Big Brother and the Thought Police monitored everyone. Big Brother is now part of our vernacular and is synonymous with unwanted eavesdropping into our private affairs. While Orwell's novel was politically motivated, he envisioned a world in which technology advanced to the point where observation of everyone and everything would be possible.

We have arrived. Our capacity to observe people, their environment, and their digital patterns would make Big Brother green with envy. However, unlike the Orwellian dystopia of the future, the data will (most likely) not be used to control the masses, but rather to connect people to the products and services they will most likely want or need.

Instant Messaging Marketing

Instant messaging has been around for a while, with apps such as Facebook Messenger, WhatsApp, Viber, and WeChat. These could be some of the most underutilized marketing channels on the internet. Have you ever noticed that when you receive a text message from a friend you open it up right away? If they include a link, you almost always click it. That's because the message is coming from a trusted source.

Millions of mobile users are using private messaging service and the numbers have been doubling each year for the past several years. Expect instant messaging marketing to become more mainstream over the next two years. This will be especially true with bots communicating through messaging services for customer acquisition, relations, and resources as the technology becomes more refined. Facebook Messenger has already started down this path.

Long-Term Future

In the technology world, five years is considered long-term. After all, that's over three technology generations away by Moore's Law standard. So, predicting where marketing and automation will be, is risky at best. However, we do see three big developments that you should watch. First, expect social media channels to become a one-stop-shop for a lot of daily activities, like socializing, entertainment, education, and job-hunting. When social media platforms first emerged, they had one major function – Facebook was for connecting with friends, YouTube was video, Twitter was texting out loud, LinkedIn was business, and Instagram was pictures. Now look at these channels – Facebook owns Instagram, introduced Messenger, has live streaming, videos, and hosts job postings. The same goes for Twitter–they broadcast NFL football games every season and have purchased Periscope, a social media platform specializing in video. As every day goes by, each major social media channel will offer more functions that overlap with each other. Expect to see the latest live event or reality show, listen to music, message friends, and anything else that involves virtual socialization and entertainment. What we call social media today will become heavily integrated into our daily lives (you haven't seen anything yet).

Social media platforms continue to add new functionality and buy up other platforms is due to one reason: competition. Social media platforms are deathly afraid of losing their market share. If another platform has a different culture or has a new functionality, it has the potential to diminish the popularity of the first platform (like Facebook did to Myspace). It could cost them billions in the not-so-long run.

This means that social media platforms have two options: beat'em or buy'em. Beating competition means expanding functionality so that users stay on their platform rather than spend time on another platform. If they can't beat the competition or it will cost more to beat the competition than the competition is worth, they will be bought. We can see an example of this when we look at Facebook's acquisition of Instagram for $1 billion, even though it was valued at around $500 million at the time. However, the ROI of the Instagram acquisition has been wonderful for Facebook. Facebook created Messenger and bought WhatsApp in the same spirit of competition. The main goal for competing platforms is to acquire as many users as possible and lose none along the way. In order to compete, they must have all of the functionality of other platforms, as well as a unique culture or purpose. We run into people all the time who "don't have a Facebook," but you certainly can "find on Instagram." Facebook is much happier to hear this than someone whose sole platform is Snapchat, which was the impetus for creating Instagram, Messenger, and Facebook Stories.

Second, the social media will consolidate into one or two major players. Expect one or two companies to dominate the market. Just like the smartphone market started with a hand full of carriers, now we have two major players, Verizon and AT&T, and a bunch of second-tier players. The same goes for phones themselves as well; we started with many variations of smartphones, but now we are divided by iPhone or Android. The consolidation has already started to happen. Google purchased YouTube, Microsoft now owns LinkedIn, Facebook purchased Instagram, and Twitter acquired Periscope and Vine. This is just the beginning.

Third, in the long-term, the vast majority of marketing automation will be driven by artificial intelligence. We've seen how marketing automations has quickly moved from email automation to an ecosystem of marketing channels. This evolution will continue as the ecosystem morphs into an artificially intelligent neural network. Neural networks are designed to model the human brain, creating a network of interconnection procedures capable of making real-time decision and then taking immediate action, similar to the nervous system in our body. Like the human brain, they can learn from the environment and detect patterns.

The digital marketing ecosystem has grown from its beginnings as email campaigns to the virtually limitless capabilities we have through social media channels and automation. The foundation has been laid, and the ecosystem will continue to evolve exponentially in the way of digital intelligence. Welcome to the jungle.

APPENDIX A CRM

Setup

1. Do you use a CRM system?
   a. Yes/No plus the name of your CRM if it is a commercial product.
2. If yes, what modules/functions do you use?
   a. Generally, CRM software comes as a basic package with the ability for customers to add more functionality for sales, marketing, services, social media, etc.
3. Do you have a database of customer/prospect information?
   a. Yes/No.
4. If yes, which database do you use?
   a. MySQL, SQL Server, Oracle, etc.
5. If yes, is it integrated with your website or any other marketing channel?
   a. This question get to the extent of your CRM automation. Are you capturing data about customer and putting it into your database - from your website, Facebook, LinkedIn, etc.
6. Are you running any marketing programs with the CRM data?
   a. Yes/No and what are they.
7. What insights have you gained from the CRM data?

a. An insight can be demographics, such as most visitors to our website are between the ages of 25-34 years old, ecommerce average purchase, or more people sign up for your newsletter within 24 hours of receiving an email.

8. Is your CRM data capture focused on customers, prospects, or both?
   a. Companies that already have lots of customers will set up their CRM, website, and social media to foster better relations with their customer and sell them more products. Therefore, you CRM will be tuned to manage current customer. If you have fewer customer and focus your attention on acquiring prospects, your CRM will be setup to capture name, contact information, and introducing your business.

9. Do you use any other customer/prospect management tools?
   a. Yes/No and what are they?

Marketing & Analytics

10. Do you capture customer/prospect information separately from your CRM?

a. Yes/No. Spreadsheets, ecommerce, social media, etc. If you do, it may mean that you will need to consolidate customer/prospect profile information from multiple source.

11. Do you use web forms, call to action, or social media like buttons to capture data?

a. Yes/No.

12. Is most of the CRM data you capture, manually entered or automated?

a. Many companies capture customer/prospect information but don't have a CRM. So, you could be capturing information but not using CRM software.

13. If yes, what information do you capture?

a. List the information.

14. If yes, does it capture social media data?

a. Yes/No and what social media data do you capture?

15. Do you use a scoring system for customers and/or prospects?

a. Yes/No.

16. Do you segment customers?

a. Yes/No. Do you place customers into some sort of grouping?

Cost & Resources

17. How much time do you spend support, using, and managing the CRM?
    a. This is the number of hours your business spends each month on the CRM.
18. What are the ongoing cost of maintaining the CRM?
    a. This is the direct cost paid to your CRM provider for service or maintenance. Business that use an online CRM Services, such as Salesforce.com, pay a monthly fee of approximately $50 per user.
19. Is there any ongoing licensing associated with the CRM?
    a. In addition to a monthly fee for the CRM, you could have other cost such as monthly payments to services that provide lists of businesses, names, and contact information.

About the Authors

Steve Thomas

Steve is a marketing automation technology consultant, specializing in software development required to automate online marketing.

He co-founded Pathlore Software Company, which introduced one of the world's first enterprise eLearning management systems. As CEO, he grew the company from inception to over $30 million in sales, 1,800+ business customers, and seven offices including Europe and Asia Pacific.

After selling Pathlore, Steve co-founded Wirefree, leading a research & development team to create web software for the emerging Internet of Things (IoT) market.

He is a past Ernst & Young Entrepreneur of the Year finalist for Technology, a graduate of The College of William & Mary, and holds a Master's Degree in Computer Science from American University in Washington, D.C.

His experience as a hands-on CTO and CEO of a web software company, lead him into the Marketing Automation business. As a consultant, he advises clients on how to use technology to grow their businesses online.

Steve lives just north of Columbus in Powell, Ohio with his wife Jana and his two school-aged boys,

Avery and Jack. He's been a lifelong golf enthusiast and trains and competes in "Pump and Run" contests.

Brian Thomas

Brian is a social media strategist and consultant who believes social media should be a fulcrum to businesses rather than an afterthought. He specializes in marketing automation systems.

He lives in Columbus, OH and is the Founder and President of Impact Social, a digital marketing firm. At Impact Social, he consults with businesses to improve their marketing practices by implementing automation systems and developing execution strategies.

Brian graduated from Virginia Tech with a B.S. in Mechanical Engineering and has since worked in business development for an IoT/Internet of Things technology development company, before starting Impact Social. His responsibility was to find problems that could be solved with IoT technology in the large manufacturing and healthcare industries. From concept to delivery, he was involved with entire lifecycle of new technology products.

In leisure, Brian enjoys travel, language, and leading a healthy lifestyle. He has been an avid snowboarder for 17 years as well as played the violin and viola since he was 6. He also volunteers his time for youth mentorship and teaching English as a second language.

Brian believes that a well thought out and executed social media strategy is the key to business success in the digital age. He is the co-author of *Marketing Automation Foundation: Eliminating Unproductive Marketing.*

References

1. [i] "The Top 20 Valuable Facebook Statistics – Updated January 2017", Zephoria Digital Media, January 2017, https://zephoria.com/top-15-valuable-Facebook-statistics/

2. [ii] 23 Reasons Why You Should Use Marketing Automation. By Marcus Taylor, https://www.ventureharbour.com/author/admin

3. [iii] https://en.wikipedia.org/wiki/LinkedIn "LinkedIn"

4. [iv] The Good, The Bad, and the future of digital marketing, Econsultancy, 11/28/2016 by Blake Cahill

5. [v] (Forbes, http://www.forbes.com/sites/kathleenchaykowski/2015/12/08/facebook-business-pages-climb-to-50-million-with-new-messaging-tools/#57cd103f1c2c)

6. [vi] (Stastista, https://www.statista.com/statistics/271258/facebooks-advertising-revenue-worldwide/)

7. [vii](Google Finance, and **https://en.wikipedia.org/wiki/Initial_public_offering_of_Facebook)**

8. [viii]https://business.facebook.com/ads/manager/pixel/facebook_pixel/?act=1329820313750238&pid=p1&business_id=1327936600605276 Setup Your Facebook Pixel by Facebook

9. [ix] https://www.emarketer.com/Article/Fashion-Brands-Strike-Pose-Instagram/1012684

10. [x] (Stastia, **https://www.statista.com/statistics/253577/number-of-monthly-active-instagram-users/)** .

11. [xi] (Wikipedia, google finance).

12. [xii] (http://fortune.com/2016/09/22/instagram-advertising-growth/)

13. [xiii] http://expandedramblings.com/index.php/important-instagram-stats/

14. https://blog.hootsuite.com/**instagram-demographics/**

15. https://www.bloomberg.com/news/articles/2016-04-19/credit-suisse-says-instagram-will-generate-over-three-times-as-much-revenue-as-facebook-paid-to-acquire-it

16. Sprout Social: http://sproutsocial.com/insights/new-social-media-demographics/#instagram

17. [xiv] (source: Nielsen's)

18. [xv]**https://business.facebook.com/ads/manager/pixel/facebook_pixel/?act=1329820313750238&pid=p1&business_id=1327936600605276** Setup Your Facebook Pixel By Facebook

19. [xvi] http://lightspandigital.com/blog/20-instagram-marketing-tips/

20. [xvii][xvii] https://business.linkedin.com/marketing-solutions/blog/s/success-story-how-holiday-inn-express-effectively-used-humor-to-reach-consumers-on-linkedin LinkedIn Marketing Solutions Blog, April 1, 2015 Success Story: How Holiday Inn Express Effectively Used Humor to Reach Consumers on LinkedIn

21. [xviii] https://business.linkedin.com/marketing-solutions/case-studies/holiday-inn-express?trk=s-bl How Holliday Inn Express Stayed Smart, LinkedIn Marketing Solutions

22. [xix] https://en.wikipedia.org/wiki/LinkedIn "LinkedIn"

23. [xx] (https://www.timetoast.com/timelines/the-history-of-youtube--4)

24. [xxi](https://en.wikipedia.org/wiki/List_of_most_viewed_YouTube_videos).

25. [xxii]https://www.slideshare.net/wearesocialsg/digital-in-2016?next_slideshow=1

26. http://www.statisticbrain.com/youtube-statistics/

27. http://images.jobcentral.com/jcv2/chad/YouTube-One-Sheet.pdf

28. [xxiii] **http://expandedramblings.com/index.php/yout ube-statistics/**

29. [xxiv] (http://expandedramblings.com/index.php/youtub e-statistics/).

30. [xxv] https://www.bing.com/videos/search?q= why+market+on+youtube&qpvt=why+mark et+on+youtube&view=detail&mid=7663D57 A7578E4F4D5197663D57A7578E4F4D519&F ORM=VRDGAR 5 reasons you should use YouTube for marketing your business June 27, 2016 by Mak Live

31. [xxvi] https://support.google.com/adwords/answ er/2545661?hl=en Google AdWords Support, About Remarketing to YouTube viewers.

32. [xxvii] (http://www.barrons.com/articles/digital-ad-growth-youtube-will-lift-alphabet-20-1484976368)

33. [xxvii] https://research.fb.com/facebook-ai-academy/ Facebook AI Academy March 29, 2017 by Larry Zitnick

Manufactured by Amazon.ca
Acheson, AB